M000209921

OF HEAVEN AND EARTH

SITCHIN STUDIES DAY

The first *Sitchin Studies Day* was held in Denver, Colorado, on October 6, 1996, as the concluding day of the 1996 International Forum on New Science held by the International Association for New Science of Fort Collins, Colorado.

This book offers the complete record of the proceedings.

Cover illustration: A 5,000-year-old Sumerian depiction of a spacecraft and astronauts. Zecharia Sitchin, in his book *The 12th Planet,* believes that the celestial symbols indicate that the space-craft is passing near Mars and its astronaut is communicating with a colleague on Earth. Sitchin says astronauts from the 12th Planet (the Biblical *Nefilim)* landed on Earth 445,000 years ago.

© Zecharia Sitchin, *The 12th Planet.*

Reproduced with permission, 1996.

OF HEAVEN AND EARTH
Essays Presented at the First Sitchin Studies Day

**EDITED BY
ZECHARIA SITCHIN**

The Book Tree
Escondido, California

Copyright © 1996 by Zecharia Sitchin and Madeleine Briskin, Marlene Evans, V. Susan Ferguson, Neil Freer, Antonio Huneeus and Charles Louis Moore, in respect to each one's essay.

All rights reserved. No part of this publication may be reproduced, stored in a retrieval system, or transmitted, in any form or by any means, electronic, mechanical, photocopying, recording, or otherwise, without the prior permission of the individual copyright holder.

Published with permission by
The Book Tree
c/o P.O. Box 724
Escondido, California 92026

Special Edition — October 1996
for Sitchin Studies Day (only 600 copies)
First Edition — November 1996

Library of Congress Cataloging-in-Publication Data

Of Heaven and Earth: Essays Presented at the First Sitchin Studies Day. Edited by Zecharia Sitchin.

ISBN 1-885395-17-5

1. Civilizations — Ancient Civilizations.   2. Human Origins.
3. Extraterrestrial Contacts.   4. Religions — origins and future.

I. Sitchin, Zecharia.   II. Briskin, Madeleine.   III.   Evans, Marlene.
IV. Ferguson, V. Susan.   V. Freer, Neil.   VI. Huneeus, Antonio.
VII. Moore, Charles Louis.

PRINTED IN THE UNITED STATES OF AMERICA
by
Kendall/Hunt Publishing Co.
Dubuque, Iowa

CONTENTS

John M. Cogswell was born in Colorado and grew up on a ranch in Kansas. He received his B.A. in history from Yale University and his L.L.B. degree from Georgetown Law Center in 1964. After service in the U.S. Marine Corps he started practicing law in Denver and Buena Vista, Colorado. His interest in the writings of Zecharia Sitchin began in 1988. He has been studying Sitchin's works intensely since then and has travelled on six international expeditions with him to witness first hand the evidence relied on in Zecharia Sitchin's seven books.

OPENING REMARKS
by
John M. Cogswell

This event, which I hope will become an annual one, brings together people who have become familiar with the writings of Zecharia Sitchin and who have begun to wonder: What if he is right? And if he is right, and the past is a clue to our future, how do we make more people aware of the significance of his findings?

This Studies Day will enable us to hear not only Zecharia Sitchin, but several other speakers, each one an expert in a particular field of work and study, whose own endeavors have been influenced, inspired or enhanced by the writings of Zecharia; and it will be my pleasure to introduce them to you in the course of this Day.

If you are anything like I am, you stumbled into this subject by accident, then read every book you could find and, in the process, became haunted for a month or so as the paradigm common to the larger part of our culture became thoroughly shattered. Somewhere in the process, you learned about Zecharia Sitchin and then read one or more of his books. You have reached that stage where you are waiting for his next book to find out some more about the truth of our past.

Following my completion of *The 12th Planet* sometime in 1992, my curiosity compelled me to track down Zecharia and speak with him. I found his phone number in the New York City Directory, called him, and congratulated him on having written so well in 1976. That phone call was the genesis of a personal friendship between Zecharia and me and six international expeditions.

In 1993 Zecharia was persuaded to accompany an Egyptian tour, and then five more tours to the Sinai, Jordan, Peru, Mexico, Greece and Crete, all of which focused on the studies of Zecharia. I have been fortunate enough to have attended all six trips and, as a result, have been privileged:

- to hear his many lectures during our travel expeditions;
- to discuss numerous subjects of interest with Zecharia;
- to find meaning in terms which previously blew over me like so much wind—terms like Sumerians, Akkadians, Babylonians, Hittites, Dorians, Olmecs, Incas, Toltecs, Aztecs, Mayans and many others.
- to be assured of Zecharia's absolute sincerity and integrity; and
- to be continually amazed at the breadth of Zecharia's knowledge and insight which even surpasses my wonderment that he is able to read at least 11 different languages, including most of the languages of our early civilizations.

I have witnessed Zecharia's excitement upon making new discoveries during our trips and have pressed him enough to pry as much as one can from this uniquely private man whose love of books, writings and the truth has enabled him to contribute so much, so thoroughly and so objectively to our knowledge of our past, and allowed those of us whose curiosity is unfathomable to seemingly have some answers to the big questions most people know nothing about.

Prying anything personal from Zecharia is a major task for, frequently, his response is "no more questions today." Nonetheless, I have been persistent and want to share a few tidbits of information that I have discovered about Zecharia.

Zecharia's story started when he was nine years old in Hebrew class in Palestine. He and his classmates were studying Noah, who he was and how he was told to build the ark. The opening biblical verse on the subject is a favorite of many Sunday school teachers because it says that those were the days when there were *giants* upon the earth, that their intermarriage with the daughters of man was mankind's downfall and that's why mankind was punished by the flood. When they got to that part of the story, Zecharia raised his hand and addressed the teacher saying, "Excuse me, my teacher, why do you say 'giants' when the word in the Bible is Nephilim which comes from the root 'Naphal' which means 'to come down,' and it says that those were the days when the Nephilim, those who come down from heaven to earth, not giants, were upon the earth?" Zecharia was expecting to be complimented for his knowledge of Hebrew but instead was told to "Sit down and do not question the Bible!"

What the Hebrew teacher did not know was that this criticism, instead of the expected compliment, would motivate Zecharia to dedicate the large part of his adult life to learn the truth about our origins. He studied and studied, traveled and traveled and talked and talked until one day his wife, Rina, said, "Isn't it time, Zecharia, that you stop talking about this subject and start writing?" Zecharia, being a journalist by trade, was used to writing articles, not books. Yet he took Rina's suggestion to heart and the result was *The 12th Planet* in 1976. When he began, he thought it would be his only book, but he has now written a total of seven and, even today, has plans for more.

If you ask Zecharia what he calls himself, he will say that he is not an author—he is not a Biblical scholar — he is not an archaeologist — he is not a linguist. He is a little bit of all of these, but mostly, he is a *reporter* because of his ability to report to us today what people thousands of years ago knew and witnessed and believed in.

Anyone who knows Zecharia and is interested in this subject could talk much longer in extolling the academic virtues and integrity of this unusual and especially intelligent man — Zecharia Sitchin — who many of us believe will one day receive a Nobel Prize.

It gives me great pleasure to introduce Zecharia in this first assembly called Sitchin Studies Day. And I know, as you listen to Zecharia and read and study his books and those of others who have pursued related subjects, that your interest in life and fascination with who you are and where you came from and possibly where you are going will grow and grow.

6

Zecharia Sitchin, one of a small number of orientalists who can read the Sumerian clay tablets which trace Earth's and human events to the earliest times, was born in Russia and raised in Palestine, where he acquired a profound knowledge of modern and ancient Hebrew and of other Semitic and European languages, the Old Testament, and the history and archaeology of the Near East. He graduated from the University of London, majoring in Economic History, having attended the London School of Economics and Political Science. He is a member of the American Association for the Advancement of Science, the American Oriental Society, the Middle East Studies Association of North America, and the Israel Exploration Society. His books, which have been translated into thirteen languages from their English originals, include *The 12th Planet* (1976), *The Stairway to Heaven* (1980), *The Wars of Gods and Men* (1985), *The Lost Realms* (1990), *Genesis Revisited* (1990), *When Time Began* (1993) and *Divine Encounters* (1996).They are available in hardcover from Bear & Co. of Santa Fe, NM, and in paperback from Avon Books.

Abstract

The recent announcement by NASA that rocks from Mars contain evidence of early life forms on that planet came on the heels of other discoveries reporting the existence of planets around other suns and of water, internal heat sources and other conditions on moons of other planets in our own solar system that are conducive to Life. Taken together, the discoveries have publicly raised the ultimate question: *Are we alone?*

The implications of an affirmative answer are immense and go beyond the realms of science. The impact on intellectual and philosophical arenas would be profound were it to be confirmed that Life is not unique to Earth. Few in the scientific, intellectual and religious circles even dare think what if such a seed of life, that has evolved on Earth to Homo sapiens, has also led to the rise of intelligent beings on other planets.

But a discussion of such a possibility and its implications has already been going on, not as an offshoot of science-fiction but on the basis of solid scientific evidence from the past. Paramount among varied evidence that much that we are discovering is really a process of *re*-discovery is the astounding knowledge recorded by the Sumerians. Their civilization blossomed out suddenly some 6,000 years ago in what is nowadays Iraq; it accounts for virtually every aspect of what we deem essential to a modern high civilization; and it displayed knowledge of the heavens with which we are only catching up.

Sumerian knowledge explains how our solar system came to be, how Mankind came to be. Its amazingly accurate answers to countless enigmas in the heavens and on Earth stemmed from the ancient assertion that We Are Not Alone.

ARE WE ALONE?
THE ENIGMA OF ANCIENT KNOWLEDGE
by
Zecharia Sitchin

As I stand here before this notable audience to introduce the first Sitchin Studies Day, I cannot avoid thoughts of vindication.

It was just a few weeks ago that NASA, the National Aeronautics and Space Administration, announced at a major press conference the discovery of evidence for life on another planet. The exhibit was a small piece of rock that was discovered in Antarctica and that presumably had reached Earth from the planet Mars a long time ago. Using instruments that were not available before, a team of scientists found within the rock evidence of minuscule living organisms that, presumably, thrived on Mars some four billion years ago.

No matter how tiny or primitive, no matter how long ago, the announcement of the discovery of such life forms outside the confines of our planet was received with worldwide interest; for, it was pointed out, that is how life on Earth had begun — from a kind of "seeds of life," one-celled, primitive, some four billion years ago. The question that sprang to mind was, Has NASA found in a rock from Mars evidence for the same process that has in time led to the appearance of Man on this planet?

Pressed to explain the significance of the discovery, Daniel S. Goldin, NASA's Administrator, took a glimpse into the future. Indeed, he conceded, the implications might be far reaching. The

Copyright © Zecharia Sitchin, 1996

ultimate question that the findings raise, he allowed, could well be the question: ARE WE ALONE?

Echoing this realization, Dr. Richard Zare of Stanford University, a member of the scientific team that studied the rock from Mars, wrote as follows in an Op-Ed article in *The New York Times:* "This could be a first step in answering the age-old question of whether we are alone in the universe and to what extent life is unique to Earth. The defining moment of the space age could well be the discovery that we are not alone in the universe."

As I was reading the headlined reports, as I was watching the news conference on television, as I heard and read the three magical words — Are We Alone? — I could not help but ask a silent question, a bitter-sweet question: What took them so long?

For it was *twenty years ago* — at this time in 1976 — that I asked that very same question, with the very same words — Are We Alone? Are We Unique? — in my book *The 12th Planet.*

Those of you who have read that first book will recall that I not only raised the question, I also proceeded to give the answer.

The Nefilim

The answer, you will recall, was not a product of my imagination. Rather, it was based on solid evidence from antiquity. Some of you have probably heard already how I had happened to embark on the search that has brought me, via seven books, to this forum.

I was a schoolboy, privileged to study the Bible in its original language, Hebrew. We reached the story of the Great Flood in the book of Genesis, where it is stated that it was at that time that the NEFILIM were upon the Earth, who went on to marry the daughters of Man. The teacher explained that the story speaks of giants who were then upon the Earth. I raised my hand and pointed out that the word literally meant those who have descended, who have come down (in the context) from the heavens to Earth. For that, instead of being complimented, I was reprimanded. "You don't question the Bible!" the teacher roared . . .

I can still feel the hurting. It caused me to become persistent in looking for the answer to the enigma of the Nefilim. To whom was the Bible referring? And why does the next verse in Genesis refer to them as sons (plural) of the gods (plural) — an aberration in a Bible devoted to monotheism?

A clue in a 19th century commentary led me to seek the answer in the mythologies of the ancient peoples. There, there had been the many gods (with a small 'g'). From Greece I traced them back across the Mediterranean Sea to the ancient Near East. The myths of the Egyptians and Assyrians, Babylonians and Hittites and Canaanites, seemed to tell the same tales, only calling the same pantheons by different names. In the end I discovered that all those myths, and thus the enigmatic verses in the Bible about the Nefilim, had a common earlier source: tales of gods and men first written down on clay tablets by a people called *Sumerians*.

The Discovery of Sumer

Up to about a century ago no one knew a thing about Sumer. The Bible did talk of a land it called *Shine'ar* , a kingdom with great cities which had preceded Assyria and Babylonia; but that was held to be a myth. Even after archaeologists had uncovered the remains of Assyria and Babylonia, taking us back 3,000 and 4,000 years, doubts remained regarding the biblical assertion that there had been cities named Erech and Akkad and Ur before Babylon and Nineveh in the plain between the Euphrates and Tigris rivers.

But the more archaeologists moved to excavate sites farther south in Mesopotamia, closer to the Persian Gulf, the older were the discovered cities. Erech was discovered, and Ur too — the city whence Abraham had come. And now we know that there had indeed been a land called Shine'ar; we call it SUMER. And it was there that Mankind's first known civilization arose, circa 4000 B.C. — long before Assyria and Babylonia, almost a millennium before the Egyptian civilization began.

Scholars speak of the Sumerian civilization's appearance as "sudden," "unexpected," "out of nowhere." All at once, without

Components of a great soc.

precedent or gradualism, there sprang up a high and manifold civilization with great urban centers, high-rise temples, palaces, courts of justice, commerce, even taxation. There were kings and priests, judges and doctors, dancers and musicians. There were irrigation, crafts, industries, metallurgy, shipping, mathematics; and above all: writing and a written language, scribes, schools, a literature, epic tales, proverbs, poems.

Archaeologists have dug up in the ruins of ancient Sumer many artful statues. In *The 12th Planet* I included illustrations of some of the ladies depicted by those statues, showing how they dressed, how their hair was done. One cannot but be impressed by their noble demeanour, their rich attire, their elaborate hairdos. It is just a glimpse of their cultured life. The clay tablets were sometimes inscribed with elaborate recipes for food preparation; I chose to quote from one for cooking chicken in wine — the French specialty of Coq-au-vin but from thousands of years ago. Recently it was discovered that a very special way of making beer in a traditional enclave in Belgium in fact employed beer-making methods specified by the Sumerians; it was there that beer and beer brewing were invented.

The First Known Civilization

Or let's look at another aspect of civilization also begun in Sumer — the concept of laws and contracts, of courts and judges. Many of you have undoubtedly heard of the Law Code of Hammurabi, the Babylonian king. But how many knew, before my writings had brought the Sumerian civilization to life, that Sumerian law codes preceded the Babylonian one by fifteen hundred years? Moreover, whereas the Babylonian code was just a list of crimes and their punishments — if you do this your punishment will be that — the Sumerian law codes were codes of justice: You shall not take away the donkey of a widow, you shall not delay the wages of a laborer. Or take their proverbs, like this one: "Man — for his pleasure, marriage; on thinking it over, divorce." Some of the poetry, such as a lullaby sung by a mother to her sick child, are unmatched by modern lyrics. Their music, scientists at Berkeley have found, was based on the same principles and used notes as we still do nowadays, except that the notes were in the cuneiform script.

In matters of technology, as in matters of social organization and cultural affairs, almost every aspect of a high civilization one can think of began in Sumer. Its "firsts" included the wheel and wheeled vehicles, boating and sails. The kiln, crucial to the making of strong bricks and to metallurgy, began there. The brick itself, still an essential part of building and urbanism, was a Sumerian first — a fact first mentioned in the Bible, in the tale of the Tower of Babel. The complex casting method called "lost wax" began there.

Advanced Sciences

As one looks at an inscribed clay tablet with its seemingly countless number of combinations of long and short lines that form the cuneiform script that was invented in Sumer, the system looks disorderly, and one wonders how the ancient scribes could have remembered all those combinations. But as I show in my book *Genesis Revisited*, these were not haphazard combinations of lines. Rather, they were very orderly and thought-out combinations that were based on sophisticated mathematical theories now known as the Ramsey Graph Theory that was first suggested by Frank R. Ramsey in 1928. It dealt with the problem of how points could be connected by lines without repetition. In my book I have shown that the Sumerian cuneiform script was based on the same principles — but thousands of years earlier.

In matters of geometry, we find that not only squares and rectangles could be measured, but also circles, triangles and various odd shapes. In fact triangulation, on which geography and and navigation on Earth as well as the measurement of celestial distances in the heavens depend, was known in Sumer. Their term for Earth was KI (of which more later} and its script sign was a flattened globe crossed by a lines-pattern, akin to the way that we show the Earth's globe with meridians across its face.

The concept of the "four corners of the Earth" and the "four winds of heaven," the cardinal points, comes to us from Sumer. Temples were built according to precise and prescribed orientations; modern archaeoastronomers have found the orientations to have been so precise that they enable us to determine when the temples were built. The earliest temples, built as stage-pyramids called ziggurats, served as astronomical observatories and were depositories of precise knowledge regarding the relationship between the motions of the Earth, the Sun and the Moon. Thus the phenomena of the equinoxes (when twice a year the Sun passes the equator) and of the solstices (when the Sun reaches its farthest points north and south) were known.

A Sophisticated Astronomy

Solstices and equinoxes, and the other aspects of the triple dance involving Earth, Moon and Sun, are of course the essential elements of the calendar. That too, the calendar, was a Sumerian first — not the notching of marks on bones to record the passing days, but a complex solar-lunar calendar that became the basis of all ensuing calendars and still in use to our times. While others have avoided the need for complex calculations to keep intact the Sun/Moon cycle that repeats itself every 19 years or so (the Christians rely solely on the solar year, the Moslems solely on the lunar year), the Jewish calendar has retained the dual nature due to the knowledge of the secret of what is called Intercalation. Indeed the Jewish calendar, which marked this past September the start of the year 5757, is precisely the Sumerian calendar begun in the sacred city called Nippur in 3760 B.C.

Much of the astronomical knowledge usually attributed to the Greeks, such as the so-called Metonic Cycle of about 19 years for the return of the Sun and Moon to their same relative positions, was thus in reality Sumerian astronomical knowledge that had reached the Greeks — mostly of Asia Minor — via "Chaldean" (late Babylonian) intermediaries. The phenomenon was called *Precession*: the slight retardation (about one degree every 72 years) in the Earth's orbit around the Sun. Textbooks usually teach you that Precession was first mentioned by the Greek Hipparchus in the

2nd century B.C. In fact, he himself wrote that he had learned of this phenomenon — hardly observable in one man's lifetime — from the Chaldeans. In my writings I show beyond doubt that the Sumerians had already known of Precession and had linked it to what we still call the start of New Ages every 2,000/2,200 years or thereabouts. It was the Sumerians who first divided the celestial circle into twelve houses of the Zodiac, who named these zodiacal constellations by names we still use, and depicted them pictorially as the Bull or the Ram or the Maiden the way we still continue to do. It was they who recorded the shift from Gemini to Taurus to Aries, and it is thus to them that we owe not only the basis for astrology, but also the current expectations of the coming of a New Age, the Age of Aquarius.

The annual calendar, recording one orbit of the Earth around its parent star, and the zodiacal calendar, recording a shift of astronomical phenomena, are examples of the marriage by the Sumerians of advanced mathematics with a sophisticated astronomy. Indeed, Sumerian knowledge in the field of astronomy is the most amazing aspect of their attainments, for it included knowledge which *we* are only now beginning to attain.

The astonishing fact is that all the principles of spherical astronomy on which modern astronomy is based, come to us from the Sumerians: the concepts of a celestial sphere, an axis, a zenith, a horizon, the plane of orbit, the circle of 360 degrees, the grouping of stars into constellations — all that and more is found in Sumerian records and in Babylonian, Assyrian or Hittite copies of the Sumerian astronomical tablets.

Secrets of Our Solar System

We learn in school that the first one to suggest that the Sun and not the Earth was in the center of our planetary system was Copernicus, in 1543. NOT SO. The Sumerians knew, and stated, that the Sun, not Earth, was in the Center and that the Sun was there long before the Earth had even come into being. Moreover, they left behind drawings of the solar system showing just that. It has been assumed all along that the ancient peoples were not aware of the planets beyond Saturn, for the simple reason that they cannot be seen without telescopes. We ourselves discovered Uranus, the one after Saturn, only in 1781, after the telescope was invented. Neptune, farther out, was discovered in 1846; and Pluto, so far out that even telescopes could hardly discern its features, was unknown until 1930. Yet the Sumerians knew about all of these distant planets!

Since *The 12th Planet* was published, a certain cylinder seal has become familiar to millions of readers. Cylinder seals were another Sumerian invention — the forerunner of our rotary presses. Craftsmen, using tools and methods that remain a mystery, cut small cylinders from hard semi-precious stones, and engraved on them *in reverse,* as a negative, images and inscriptions. The cylinder was then rolled on wet clay, impressing a positive on the clay. When the clay dried, it became a permanent depiction. Literally thousands of those cylinder seals or their impressions have been discovered; and I have studied and examined a good many of them.

It was the custom to embellish the depictions with images of celestial bodies at the top. Favorites were the Sun or the Moon, or Venus. One day I came upon a cylinder seal in the museum in what was then East Berlin, cataloged under the number VA/243. Incredibly, it showed a complete solar system, with a rayed Sun — not the Earth — in the center, and all the planets we know of nowadays in the correct order and relative sizes! The date of this cylinder seal is circa 2500 B.C. — more than 4,500 years ago; and it does show Uranus and Neptune and Pluto.

Well before the fly-by of the spacecraft Voyager-2 at Neptune in August 1989, I had predicted what its instruments will see and learn about that distant planet. It will be blue-green, with odd-colored patches on its surface, akin in many respects to Uranus, and — a most audacious prediction — *watery.* I was right in all of those predictions. How could I have known? Because the *Sumerians* had known. In my very first book, *The 12th Planet,* I quoted Sumerian descriptions of all the planets, including Uranus and Neptune. When Voyager-2 flew by Uranus in 1986, I literally jumped out of my seat and shouted, "Oh my God, but that is exactly how the Sumerians had described it!" They called Uranus "the twin of Neptune" and thus I could predict what NASA eventually discovered about Neptune.

The Sumerians asserted repeatedly that "the family of the Sun has twelve members." They said that that family consisted of the Sun (in the center); the Moon (for reasons which they gave); and *ten* — not nine — planets. The depiction on seal VA/243 indeed shows such a *twelve* member solar system. It shows a substantial planet between Mars and Jupiter. Nowadays we do not see there a planet, but we do see the remains of a planet — the myriad fragments called the Asteroid Belt, the "hammered bracelet" in the words of the Book of Genesis. Modern astronomers are still stymied by the enigma of this circle of orbiting asteroids; but the Sumerians knew the answer to the puzzle.

A Cosmology of Creation

The Sumerians not only knew so much about the complete solar system; they also had a cosmogony that explains many of the phenomena that still baffle modern science in astronomy, geology and other disciplines. Why does Uranus lie on its side? The explanation is "a mighty bang;" but from what? Why does Triton, Neptune's largest moon, have a retrograde orbit, clockwise rather than anti-clockwise as is common in our solar system? And what had swept it into such an orbit? What pull snatched Pluto from being a satellite of an outer planet, and gave it a highly inclined and peculiar orbit? Why does Earth have a satellite, our Moon, that is much too large as planet-to-moons ratios go? What caused the mighty collision whose marks the Moon still bears? And, here on Earth, why did all the continents once congregate on one side, leaving an immense cavity that is still the Pacific Ocean on the other side? Why is the Earth's crust unevenly distributed? And how could life on Earth begin so soon, just a few hundred million years after Earth was created?

Incredibly, the Sumerians provided plausible answers to all these nagging enigmas. They did so in a variety of written texts, some of which are called by other scholars "myths" and sometimes held to be "religious texts." The longest and most hallowed of those Sumerian texts was one, known best by the opening words of its Babylonian version, *Enuma elish;* it is often referred to in scholarly books as the Mesopotamian Epic of Creation.

It was in 1876, exactly 100 years before my first book, *The 12th Planet,* was published, that George Smith, who worked in the British Museum, published a sensational work titled *The Chaldean Genesis.* Piecing together broken tablets that had been discovered in Nineveh in the library of the Assyrian king Ashurbanipal, Smith showed convincingly that there had existed in Mesopotamia a creation text relating how the Earth and the Asteroid Belt had come to be, and how Man on Earth has been created. It was a tale not unlike the one in the Bible; except that it preceded the Book of Genesis by hundreds, even thousands, of years.

In 1902 L.W. King, also of the British Museum in London, deciphered even older creation tales, and specifically one that was written on seven tablets. He titled his book *The Seven Tablets of Creation;* it was a tale that evoked the biblical seven days of creation. It was a text clearly based on a Sumerian original.

Scholars treat these texts as myths, or even as a mere allegorical tale. But in fact, as my analysis has shown, the Sumerian creation texts constitute a sophisticated cosmogony. Like the first chapters of Genesis, which in fact are an abbreviated version of the Sumerian text, it is based on highly scientific knowledge, including recognition of Evolution.

Modern science asserts that our planetary system resulted from the coalescing of primeval matter whirling around our star, the Sun — first the rockier components closer to the Sun, then the lighter and more gaseous ones farther out. The Sumerian tale calls the Sun APSU — "The one who was there from the beginning." And it reports that first to be created from the primeval cloud whirling around the Sun were its "messenger" (the planet we call Mercury) and another planet called TIAMAT.

In time, the other members of our solar system were brought about, in pairs. In the space between the Sun and Tiamat, the pair we call Venus and Mars were added. In the space beyond Tiamat, the pairs we call Jupiter and Saturn, and Uranus and Neptune coalesced. With the passage of time, some of these planets acquired their own satellite moons; Tiamat, for example, had an "assembly" of eleven; and the largest of them, called KINGU in the Sumerian text, began to veer toward its own solar orbit.

The Appearing of Nibiru

Into that newly formed and still unstable solar system there appeared, about four billion years ago, an Invader. It was a sizeable celestial body, a planet from another part of the cosmos somehow ejected from its own solar system into the vastness of space. Reaching the environs of our solar system, it began to succumb to the gravitational pull of our outer planets. The ancient text describes the dramatic change of course and the increasing attracting of the Invader into the heart of our solar system. In doing so, it caused collisions, tiltings, and the appearance of more moons — obtaining at the same time seven of its own.

As I show in *The 12th Planet,* and later on in the companion book *Genesis Revisited*, the series of occurrences described in the ancient text explain satisfactorily such puzzles "out there" as why Uranus is tilted on its side, how Pluto was pulled off from being a satellite to become a planet with the odd orbit, and so on.

With its course curving increasingly toward the center of our solar system, the Invader — travelling in a trajectory opposite to that of our planetary system — was now advancing toward an inevitable collision with Tiamat. The ancient text then describes in dramatic terms what it calls the Celestial Battle, in the course of which Tiamat's life was extinguished. One half of her was smashed into bits and pieces, to become the Asteroid Belt and comets. The other half was thrust into a new orbit, closer to the Sun — to become planet Earth. The Sumerians called Earth KI — the Cleaved One, from which comes the Greek Gaea and the prefix "Geo" for geography, geometry etc. in English. This cosmogony, better than any theory in modern science, explains why Earth started with an immense gap or wound on one side (that is still the deep and vast Pacific Ocean), why all the continents were once together on one side, and why our Moon is unusually large as a planetary satellite: for it is none other than Kingu, the largest satellite of Tiamat, that was pulled with the future Earth to the new orbit.

And what happened to the Invader? According to the ancient text, it was caught into permanent orbit around our Sun — becoming the *twelfth member* of our solar system. It was this planet that appears in the Sumerian cylinder seal passing between Mars and Jupiter, the site of the Celestial Battle. With an orbit that the Sumerians called SAR — a term that denoted both "ruler, the supreme" and the number 3,600 — this new member of the family of the Sun keeps crossing and recrossing the Asteroid Belt, where Tiamat once had been. Therefore did the Sumerians name it NIBIRU, meaning "Planet of the Crossing;" and the symbol for it was the sign of the cross.

The ancient text, told as a tale of celestial gods that come into being, jostle or annoy each other, acquire assemblies of satellites, and end up with a major celestial battle, which has become known, as I have mentioned, during the past one hundred years. Invariably, it has been considered a myth, an allegory, a literary text. The Babylonians, nearly two thousand years after the Sumerians, adopted and adapted the tale and replaced the Invader's name with that of their national god, Marduk. The text, *Enuma elish*, was read in public as the highlight of the New Year festival as a core of Babylonian religious beliefs in the supremacy of Marduk. Thus, another way scholars have looked at the text was to deem it a religious concoction intended to make Marduk also a celestial god besides his dominion on Earth. The recognized fact that the beginning of the biblical Book of Genesis echoes the *Enuma elish* only reinforced, in many minds, the religious nature of the ancient tale.

But I have seen in the text, especially when studied alongside other Sumerian and later Mesopotamian texts, a *cosmogony* — and one based on highly advanced and sophisticated scientific knowledge; a text that answers virtually all the puzzles that have baffled, and still baffle modern science regarding the creation of our solar system and others like it in the universe, the origin of the Earth and the Moon, the origin of life on Earth, of Evolution, of Mankind. And, in passing — an explanation for the enigmas on Mars and on other members of our solar system.

A Unified Theory

The tale of an Invader that re-arranged our solar system and ended up being part of it can be considered as a Unified Theory about our solar system on the one hand, and as a cosmogony embracing universal phenomena on the other hand. Take, for example, the issue of whether there are other solar systems out there. Logically and by laws of probability modern astrophysicists have surmised that among the billions of billions of stars in the universe, some act as suns surrounded by planets. But it was only in the last year or so that astronomers have concluded, with the aid of advanced instruments and satellites, that in at least three instances such outer planetary systems do exist.

But isn't that what the Sumerians have said and known thousands of years earlier? They described Nibiru as a renegade planet ejected from another solar system somewhere else in space . . .

Or take the matter of planetary moons. Until Galileo discovered with his telescope the four brightest moons of Jupiter, who could conceive that a planet could possibly have more than one companion? After the Pioneer and Voyager space missions we know that Jupiter has 16 moons, Saturn as many as 15, that both Uranus and Neptune have multiple moons. Yet we read in a text composed millennia ago that Tiamat had 11 moons and Nibiru 7. The inconceivable was known.

Compressing the Sumerian text, the Bible retained the statement that the "Firmament," the Asteroid Belt, separated the Upper Waters from the Lower Waters, and no one could understand what was meant. Until rather recently it was thought that Earth alone has water; now we know that there is water on moons of Jupiter, in the rings of Saturn, on Uranus and Neptune — indeed, water Above the Firmament; and there is or was water on Mars, and Venus, and even Mercury — indeed, water Below the Firmament.

Let us step back for a moment from such detailed examination of the insights of Sumerian cosmogony, and approach the subject from the perspective of scientific theology (for that is what, in truth, stubbornly-held scientific dogmas are). Until not long ago, cosmogony and astrophysics were dominated by a concept known as *Uniformitarianism*. It held that once the universe was created, once the solar system was created, that is how things remained. It was only a decade or so ago that a counter theory began to be seriously considered. Called *Catastrophism*, and focusing on our own solar system, it held that things were not as when they had taken shape; rather, that catastrophic events reshaped and changed our solar system. This serious look at Catastrophism was brought about by the findings of Luis Alvarez, a Nobel prizewinner, and his son Walter Alvarez — that a huge asteroid or comet struck the Earth some 65 million years ago, creating such havoc that it caused the end of the dinosaurs (the end of the Cretaceous period).

Resistance to this new concept continued fiercely, even though other scientists managed to pinpoint the location — at the tip of the Yucatan peninsula in Mexico — where the impact occurred. Resistance petered out, however, when catastrophism-in-action took place before our very eyes, when the comet Shoemaker-Levy crashed into Jupiter in July 1994. Its fragments smashed into Jupiter with a combined force equal to 500 times the combined force of all the nuclear explosions conducted on Earth since Hiroshima. The realization that catastrophic crashes happen in our solar system not as exceptions but as constant or repeated phenomena has by now led to suggestions that other extinctions on Earth, and other huge craters or mysterious impacts (like the one in Siberia in 1908), were the result of interplanetary chaos.

Come to think of it, NASA's latest announcement could not have taken place without the acceptance of catastrophism; for what did NASA say? It said that some 16 million years ago an asteroid or comet crashed into Mars with such force, that pieces of the planet flew off its surface, were thrust away, travelled in space, and some 13,000 years ago — attracted by Earth's gravitation — fell in Antarctica.

NASA and the Tenth Planet

Does this mean that NASA, or establishment astronomers, are ready to follow in my footsteps, accept Sumerian texts as scientific treatises, and acknowledge the existence of Nibiru?

Things would have probably been easier for all concerned — including me — were I to say that Nibiru was not a planet, and of some considerable size, but rather just *a comet*. Astronomers and astrophysicists are cognizant of comets with long orbital periods. A comet named Kohoutek that was seen several years ago was estimated to have an orbital period of 75,000 years. A recent comet, that is now behind the Sun but will come back into our view, comet Hale-Bopp, is estimated to have an orbit of 3,500 years — almost identical to that of the SAR orbit of Nibiru. It is also believed to be of an unusually large size — almost a miniplanet if one accepts the maximal estimates.

Many of the comets appear from the distant reaches of the solar system — from outer space, for all practical purposes, and make the turn around the Sun at a distance that, on the average, is that of where the Asteroid Belt is. Many of those comets — including the famous Halley's Comet — have retrograde orbits: they orbit the Sun not counterclockwise as the planets do, but clockwise — the way Nibiru orbits. So were I to say that Nibiru was a comet, agreement with my conclusions would have come easier.

Even my contention that Sumerian texts indicate that Nibiru was a *planet* would have been easier to swallow, were I not to say more about it . . . In fact, astronomers have speculated about the possible existence of one more planet beyond Pluto. They call it "Planet X," meaning both the unknown planet and the tenth planet (Nibiru, let me remind you, is a *tenth* planet as planets go, but the *twelfth member* of our solar system when the Sun and Moon are counted in). Astronomers in various parts of the world have searched for this planet. Notable among them was Dr. Robert S. Harrington of the United States Naval Observatory (an arm of the U.S. Department of Defense). He made his conviction of the planet's existence, and that I and my Sumerian and biblical sources are right, in an on-camera interview with me for my documentary "Are We Alone?" In my book *Genesis Revisited* I have reported various official findings indicating that Planet X not only exists, but was actually found back in 1983. Yet the official U.S. attitude has been to play down the evidence, the findings, and the subject; and efforts to pinpoint "Planet X" continue, indirectly, mostly elsewhere.

Why the reluctance, the refusal to admit the facts, to oppose further findings or disclosures?

The Problem of the Anunnaki

The answer can be summed up in one word: The ANUNNAKI. In Sumerian the word meant "Those who from heaven to Earth came." The Bible, as I have pointed out in my latest book *Divine Encounters,* rendered the term *Anakim*; and the Bible explained several times that the *Nefilim* — those "sons of the gods" who had launched me on my search — were counted among the Anunnaki. Distinguished from the Sons of Adam but yet compatible with the Daughters of Man, they were the people of the rocketships. They had come down to Earth from the heavens. They were, in current parlance, EXTRATERRESTRIALS.

And, in the scientific establishment, this word is taboo.

When Pluto was discovered in 1930, the fact that there was one more planet in our solar system was accepted and hailed; but apart from the need to change textbooks, the discovery was of no great consequence to the man in the street, to our daily lives or beliefs. The problem regarding "Planet X" is quite different . . .

The reason, you see, is that the only way to explain the enigma of the incredible Sumerian knowledge is to accept their own explanation: All that we know, they wrote, was taught to us by the Anunnaki. And the Anunnaki, they said, came down to Earth from Nibiru!

Their comings and goings between their planet and Earth began, as I gathered from the Sumerian texts, almost 450,000 years ago. Capable of space travel already then, they also possessed at least (and perhaps more) of what *we* know today. Without telescopes and microscopes, spacecraft and spectrometers, and computers and the other wizardly instruments that we have attained in the last few decades or at most a century or two, there was no way for the Sumerians to know all that they have known and recorded.

To the long list of "firsts" and advanced knowledge, let me add another puzzle. We refer to Earth as the third planet from the Sun: we count Mercury, Venus, Earth. But in Sumerian astronomical texts Earth was called the *seventh*. It was depicted, on stelas and cylinder seals, by the sign of seven dots. Now, who would even think of Earth as the seventh planet? Only, I have suggested, someone coming *into* our solar system from the other end: to someone counting from the outside in, Pluto would be the first, Neptune the second, Uranus the third, Saturn the fourth, Jupiter the fifth, Mars the sixth, and Earth — the planet that had gold — the seventh.

The Celestial Cycles

Or, let us take a quick look at Sumerian mathematics.

The Sumerian numbering system is called sexagesimal, meaning "based on sixty" (ours is called decimal, based on 10). Thus, when the digit for the number one was in the first column, it stood for one; but when shifted to the second column it represented sixty. "2" in the first column meant two; "2" in the second column meant 2x60, i.e. 120. In our system, "1" is one in the first column, ten in the second.

As a base number, 60 is more readily divisible than 10 or 100: it can be divided by 2,3,4,5,6 and no less importantly by the number 12. This was very important in Sumerian times, because the number twelve was an essential number in time-keeping (the day was divided into twelve double-hours), in the calendar (twelve months), in measurements (we still retain to this day the 12 inches in a foot), in astronomy (where the heavens were divided into twelve houses of the zodiac) and so on and on. The significance of the number twelve was reflected and retained in antiquity in other areas, such as social organization (the twelve tribes of Israel) and religious ones (the twelve disciples of Jesus).

We have retained to this day not only the significant subdivision into twelve, but also the basic Sumerian sexagesimal number 60. How else account for the fact that we divide the hour into sixty minutes, a minute into sixty seconds?

If we now shift our gaze from division to multiplication, we find that the base number 60, when multiplied by 6, gives us the number 360 which is the *arbitrary* number into which a circle is divided. Multiplying 360 by 10, we obtain the square of 60 and the number 3,600 — the SAR, the number representing Nibiru and its orbit.

Key cycles in Sumerian cosmogony, and in the affairs of the Anunnaki, were counted in and related to this SAR. A crucial period in Sumerian prehistory, in the prehistory of the Earth, was the number 432,000 (which represented 3,600 times 120). It was a number connected with the catastrophic event recalled by Mankind as the Deluge. In Hindu traditions, this number and multiples thereof defined divine ages and cataclysmic cycles on Earth. The ultimate cycle, the so-called "Day of the Lord Brahma," equalled 4,320,000,000 Earth years — coincidentally, the estimated age of our solar system; it was a number arrived at by multiplying 3,600 by 120 by 1,000 by 10. There are other instances in other peoples' lore as well as in Earth sciences, where 3,600 and multiples thereof seem to be the determining numbers.

Nibiru's Central Role

Indeed, it has been my firm belief that the orbital period of Nibiru and the Anunnaki who had come to Earth from it, lie at the core of the amazing Sumerian mathematics. Only the presence of the Anunnaki, and their role as teachers of the Sumerians, can begin to explain the sexagesimal system. It was built by progressing from 6 through a multiplication by 10 to 60; then 60 was multiplied by 6, to give us the all-important number 360. This in turn was multiplied by 10, to arrive at the SAR (3,600), and so on: a series of 6 by 10 by 6 by 10 etc. etc. Now, we can reason that 10 comes from the human number of fingers on both hands. But where does the 6 come from?

Some scholars who have studied the Mesopotamian mathematical tablets have been struck by the fact that the number 1,296,000 (the length, incidentally, of the Hindu Golden Age), is listed as a prime number from which certain divisions begin. The number, I have suggested in my book *When Time Began*, can be understood only in terms of familiarity with the phenomenon of Precession. With a retardation in Earth's orbit amounting to 1 degree in 72 years, the complete cycle encompassing 360 degrees — when the Earth returns to its original position in relation to the Sun and the zodiacal constellations — thus lasts 25,920 years. 1,296,000 represents this Grand Cycle (some call it the Platonian Year) multiplied by 50; and fifty, you might recall, was the biblical Jubilee.

But 1,296,000 is also the SAR, the orbital period of Nibiru, multiplied by 360 — the number of degrees in the Great Circle. Is there, I asked myself, a connection?

It was then that it dawned on me that I was looking at the secret of the sexagesimal system. I imagined the Anunnaki, coming from a planet whose one year (i.e. one orbit around the Sun) equals 3,600 orbits of the Earth, wishing for some more reasonable scale for relating the two orbits to one another. They discovered Precession. Dividing the celestial circle around the Sun into *twelve* parts, they create the zodiac and the zodiacal ages, lasting (mathematically) 2,160 years each (72 x 30 degrees). Now they have a more reasonable scale between the two orbits: 3,600 to 2,160. It is a ratio of 10:6 — the basis of the sexagesimal system. No wonder the ancients applied this ratio in architecture as the Golden Section, and considered its reciprocal (6:10) as the Golden Number.

The Seed of Life

So whichever way we look at it, the basic tenet of the Sumerians — the existence of Nibiru, and of the Anunnaki, is corroborated.

But to say that Planet X exists is more than tantamount to saying that the Anunnaki exist. For the same Sumerian creation tales — echoed in the Book of Genesis — also dealt with the origin of

Life and the Creation of Man. They said that the "seed of life" was brought into our solar system by Nibiru, transferred by it to Earth as a result of the collision with Tiamat.

It was therefore that life, springing from that seed, evolved along similar lines on both planets — but much earlier on Nibiru. If the collision had occurred four billion years ago, and the start on Nibiru was ahead by even one percent, life would have begun to evolve on Nibiru 40 *million* years earlier than on Earth. No wonder then that when the Anunnaki had arrived on Earth about half a million years ago, they found on Earth early hominids while they could already travel in space.

The Bible quotes in connection with the decision to bring about "the Adam" — literally, the Earthling — an entity called the *Elohim* saying: Let US make the Adam in OUR image and after OUR likeness." The Sumerian texts describes how the *Anunnaki,* in need of workers to work for them in the gold mines, decided to jump the gun on Evolution on Earth and, by mixing their genes with that of the primitive hominids, bring about *us — Homo sapiens.*

This, my friends, is the reason for holding back the truth regarding the Planet X and who is — or at least was — on it. For the political, social, religious, philosophical and intellectual implications of such an acknowledgement are immense.

NASA has taken a careful step in that direction in its announcement about "seeds of life" on Mars, and another risky step by admitting that this leads to the question, Are We Alone?

The Implications

But some trailblazers in the academic, religious and literary fields have been more courageous. They did not wait for NASA to give them the green light. Accepting the only plausible answer to the enigma of ancient knowledge, they set out to examine its implications.

Some of them will be addressing you today. They will express *their own opinions*, their own viewpoints. Their sole connection to "Sitchin" is that they have accepted the validity of my evidence and used it as a starting point for their own research, teaching and writing. Please join me in saying to them: THANK YOU.

Father Charles Moore is group leader of the Gathering of the Way. He graduated from Stanford University (AB 1949, LLB 1951), is admitted to practice law in California, and was elected District Attorney of Santa Cruz County in 1954. He was ordained a Roman Catholic Priest in 1964 and holds degrees in philosophy and theology from Catholic University. He studied Latin at a Benedictine monastery and Greek at a Jesuit seminary. He has traveled extensively in search of the ancient roots of religious practice. His avocation is language: he has studied Spanish, French, Italian, German, Welsh, Russian, and Japanese. He is acquainted with Sanskrit, Chinese, Rumanian, Turkish, Dutch, Hawaiian, and several Native American languages such as Sioux, Blackfoot, and Hopi.

Abstract

The effects of the reality of the gods. Definition of orthodoxy. Meaning of orthodoxy. Sitchin's starting point. The Nefilim (who come down). The Igigi (who watch). The Sitchin hypothesis: The gods are real. Responsibility of the gods. Relationship of the gods to God. The angel of the Exodus. Science, evolution, the origin of science. The meaning of the "ME". The return of the gods. The "alien" connection. The identity of Moses' God. The pagan god connection. The matter of prayer and telepathy. Orthodoxy in relation to telepathy and prayer. Orthodoxy and the position of the gods. The relationship of angels. The nature of the gods, yom kippur, Hazazel and the demons. The tree of knowledge and its meaning. The tree of life and eternal life. How the awareness of the gods strengthens orthodoxy. The effects of the reappearance of the gods. In praise of Eridu.

THE ORTHODOX CONNECTION

by

Father Charles Louis Moore
B.A., A.B., J.D., S.T.B.

What if the gods are real?

If they are, the whole of what we have learned as history is deeply altered, but not proven wrong.

What if the gods are real? The whole of what we have learned as religion is deeply altered, but not proven wrong.

What if the gods are real? All we have believed of God is deeply altered, but not proven wrong.

The Meaning of Orthodoxy

What is orthodoxy? The word means ortho-straight, doxos-teaching. Orthodoxy, both religious and scientific, is the hard core of everything we have been taught and hopefully have learned, both scientific and religious.

Religious orthodoxy is far more diverse than scientific orthodoxy, but each of us has been deeply influenced by whatever form of orthodoxy our environment has exposed us to. And what we have absorbed of the orthodox teaching has deeply affected our

Copyright © Charles Louis Moore, 1996

sense of values, our sense of meaning, and, most of all, our sense of self-worth.

Moreover, we are all children of the great divorce — between science and religion. Humpty Dumpty has fallen off the wall and none of our efforts have sufficed to put him together again. But perhaps if we journeyed back in time to a place where Humpty was still together and saw what he really looked like, we could find out how to reconcile our "Parents," Science and Religion. It is to just such a place in the past that Zecharia Sitchin invites us, and it may turn out that it is not a place in the past at all but a place that is still present.

"Questioning" the Bible

Zecharia Sitchin is one of a very few people who have had access to the records of earth's first civilization, and one of even fewer men who have gone to the trouble of learning the language in which they were written. He is a believing Jew and very much a part of Jewish history. He has spent his life on something that happened in his youth: the real meaning of certain words in Genesis — Hebrew words. The English translation of one word is "sons of God." the Hebrew word is Nefilim. It does not mean sons of God. It means "those who came down." It turns out that this is a segment of a lost book of scripture called the Book of Noah. A larger segment of that book has been found in Ethiopia: in the Book of Enoch. In this book also there is a reference to "those who came down." There is also a reference to the Igigi, the watchers referred to by Mr. Sitchin.

When he questioned his teacher about the translation, the teacher agreed that his translation was correct and that "Nefilim" comes from the verb *naphal*, a very renowned verb in the Hebrew language, and that *naphal* has the sense of coming or going down, but he would not elaborate on why the translation "sons of God" was used. There are other problematical texts in Genesis which have long been a puzzlement to biblical scholars, and the more deeply one probes into the original Hebrew texts the more problematical they become. For instance the Tower of Babel. In the texts concerning that famous tower in Shinaar — the modern Iraq — humans are said to have commenced to build a tower to go up to the heavens. To do so they made a "shem." The word *shem* is translated "name" and gives this rendering: "They made a name for themselves." But Sitchin points out that the word "shem" also means a rocket of some sort. It would seem that a missile is a far more relevant device than a "name" if one wishes to storm the heavens!

In the same texts God is constantly referring to God's self in the plural: e.g. "What shall *we* do?" (to keep these humans from coming up where *we* are?) and ''Let us confuse their tongues."

And of course the name of the creator God in the first line of Genesis is not "Yahweh" (YHVH) but *Elohim,* a curious word. Its singular is Eloah, meaning Goddess or Oak tree, but it is given in the plural — and not only the plural, but the masculine plural. A feminine word with a masculine plural? Intriguing.

In his latest book Zecharia Sitchin points out another long-standing problem with the first line of Genesis. It begins with the letter Beth which is the second letter of the Hebrew alphabet, a letter that means "house." There is something odd about that. A Hebrew text about creation should begin with Aleph the first letter of the Hebrew alphabet, a letter that means God for three reasons. One: It is about God. Two: It is about beginnings, Three: It is customary in Hebrew writing to align not only the words with their meaning but also the letters. The first letter should be Aleph. Where did it go? Present text: Be reshit bara Elohim et ha shamayim w et ha eretz. Meaning in English: "In the beginning God created the heavens and the earth." Probable original text: Ab rashit bara elohim, et ha shamayim w et ha eretz. Meaning in English: The Father of Beginnings created the gods, the heavens and the earth.

A major constitutional amendment? Obviously.

Who were the "gods?"

There is a great deal more of this sort of thing. It leads Mr. Sitchin to his reasonable question: Is Genesis written about the gods? If so, who are these gods? Are they angels? Are they the pagan gods? Are they the Vedic gods? And if so, what is the relationship between these "gods" and God? And where can I find out more about them?

This began his search, a search that led him across the mountain ranges of many languages, across the wide spaces of the origin of archaeology, and finally on a journey into the homeland of Father Abraham and to the city of Ur in the land of Edin.

The inhabitants of that land in the time of Abraham were the Sumerians. It now appears that if they are not the world's first civilization, they are at least the world's first civilization since the flood — that is, since that great catastrophe that ended the last ice age about 13,000 years ago.

The good news is that the Sumerians have left us a massive amount of written information about themselves in the ruins of their cities. The bad news is that all of that information is in Sumerian language, and there may be only about a handful of people in the world who can read it. The fortunate thing is that Zecharia Sitchin is one of them.

Sumerian Literature

Some of the Sumerian literature is in the usual history books: The Epic of Gilgamesh (the original story of the quest of the Grail) and the *Enuma elish* (the original of the creation story in Genesis.) These, however, usually come to us through their Babylonian redactors rather than their Sumerian originals. But the Sumerian originals do exist and they are, of course, much older.

How much older? We find a clue in the Jewish calendar. The Christian calendar gives us 1996 years since the birth of Christ (Actually it is now known to be incorrect — Christ was most probably born about 6 B.C. which would make this year 2002). The Jewish calendar gives us 5756 — the Rabbis usually say the beginning point is the day of Creation. The Sumerians give us very nearly the same number 5756, but they say it is since the first "Independence Day" when the gift of kingship "came down from the heavens" and human beings first received the right to govern themselves.

Perhaps the most challenging of the Sumerian revelations is the ME, (Pronounced "Meh"). These may be seen as the prototypes of what the Church calls "Revelation." They contain all the sciences and the essentials of religion as well. In a sense the ME are double tablets because all the sciences are balanced with their correlatives: Astronomy with Astrology, Mathematics with Numerology, Physics with Metaphysics, Chemistry with Alchemy, etc. It should be noted that one aspect is "exterior," having to do with the observed phenomena and the other is "interior," having to do with the inner processes of the observer. Modern Physics has come across a parallel relationship in the discovery (or Copenhagen interpretation) of quantum mechanics. The ME are said to have been given by the gods, like the Vedas. They may account for what the archaeologists call the mysterious "Jump Start" of our civilization. Their correlative in Judeo-Islamo-Christianity is of course the Mosaic double tablets of the Law — the Torah.

These and a great many other even more fascinating probabilities emerge from the work of Zecharia Sitchin. But in reading him we must realize that his work is not dogmatic but speculative, and his approach is hypothetical, not definitive.

The Sitchin Hypothesis

To briefly summarize Sitchin's hypothesis, it is this: The gods are real and they are responsible for both the origin of the human race as we know it and for the advent of our civilization. But god is spelled with a small g.

I once asked Mr. Sitchin: When are the gods coming back? He answered: What makes you think they even left? I also asked him another question: Is the God whom we worship the God whom the gods worship? He answered, after a moment's thought: "Yes, exactly."

In other words God and the gods are not mutually contradictory, but are related in what we might call agency. Agency, that is, in regard to us, with God as principal and gods as agents. More or less like angels, and perhaps devils.

I always wondered from my earliest years why in the book of Exodus there is an unexplained interchange between the use of the word God and the word angel. Since an angel is a messenger it is now plain that the author of Genesis did not always distinguish between the principal and the agent. And though God is clearly the ultimate cause in the mind of the writer, angel (or god) is more in the nature of immediate cause of creation and revelation (as in Exodus).

Religion and Science

All this concerns religious orthodoxy, but it also concerns scientific orthodoxy. The scientific concern involves both evolution and the origin of the science. I should remark here that though we think of the resistance that might be offered by religious orthodoxy, the resistance by adherents of scientific orthodoxy is frequently more intense. This is most clear in the case of archaeology in which academic orthodoxy is frequently defended to the point of inquisition and excommunication.

For the scientist the agency of the gods in doing the genetic experiments and cross-breeding between "earth people" and "sky people" is bound to be a challenge, but more challenging still is the discovery that the real contents of the original "revelation," the so called "ME," are literally a roster of the sciences produced with great particularity. It should be of some solace to know that the contents of these "ME" produce few surprises and are perfectly consonant with the particulars of our present scientific development.

In some respects the advent of the gods produces almost instant enlightenment as it does in explaining the astonishing antiquity of the zodiac with its remarkable orientation to the precession of the equinoxes — a phenomenon that cannot be observed in three or four human lifetimes.

Perhaps one of the most interesting challenges produced by the records concerning the gods concerns the return of the gods, or should I say the visible return of the gods. This concern crosses the frontier between religious and scientific orthodoxy. Mr. Sitchin tells us that the planet of the gods, Nibiru by name, (the word means "planet of the crossing") returns to the vicinity of earth every 3600 years. Such returns seem to be associated with the reappearance of the gods in public form. It is interesting to speculate what bearing this has on the cyclic return of saviors — Christ for Christians, Messiah for Jews, Maitreya for Buddhists, Quetzalcoatl for Meso-Americans.

And for the scientist? Obviously the questions posed by the ever increasing frequency of reports of landings from outer space could be a matter of concern for us all.

The God of Moses

In his latest book, *Divine Encounters,* Mr. Sitchin has investigated what surely is the primary concern of religious orthodoxy: Who is the God of Moses?

The author makes it plain that Moses' God in a 40-year theophany appeared the way gods had appeared in the past, but never before or since has there been a recorded appearance so long or so detailed. He also makes it clear that this God does not fit any of the descriptions of earlier gods, and that the claim of this god to be the God of gods is entirely consistent. Thus the basis of Judeo-Christiano-Islamic orthodoxy is not threatened but supported.

As regards other religions which are ancient, such as Hinduism and so-called "Paganism," it appears that they have a basic agreement concerning the gods: there are generations of the gods, there are always twelve on the high council, and they take an interest in human affairs. More interestingly, they respond to prayer.

The matter of prayer may be the second primary concern of religious orthodoxy. From the scientific side we are forced to look scientifically at what may be called the quantum aspect, more particularly extrasensory perception, specifically what we call mental telepathy. I do not recall that Mr. Sitchin addresses this subject. In fact, he seems to avoid it, probably because of its highly controversial nature. He no doubt believes that the materials he does present concerning the gods are controversial enough . . .

Prayer, Miracles, Angels

I have learned from other sources, however, that there is a great deal of material on the gods and on invocation, prayer, intervention, and miracles.

I was once asked whether it was true that the church disbelieves in mental telepathy. I answered: I know what you mean, but if they do disbelieve in it, then what are they doing when they pray? If prayer is essentially telepathic, then it appears that the gods are greatly advanced not only in technology but in the use of extrasensory phenomena, particularly telepathy.

One can almost feel the ire of Orthodox establishments concerning such a proposition. But it seems to me it is unwarranted. A re-reading of Exodus is required: "Thou shalt have no other gods before me." In other words stop sending your telepathy to the gods, and send it to the God who made them. That seems to be a safe orthodox position.

Another matter of concern is the matter of angels. Popularly angels are wholly good feathered beings with cherubic faces who respond to people's needs in various positive ways. But more theologically viewed, "angel" comes from the Greek "Angelos" meaning messenger. These messengers are sent by Moses' God to perform many if not all the tasks which God wishes performed, and in addition some of them are disobedient and dangerous. Then they are called devils. The gods fit the theological part of the description perfectly. But they are presented as being more like us: they are good folks, but have a dark side and are quite capable of error and go to war. They are not particularly unfriendly on the whole, but most of them are more or less indifferent to the human situation, being more concerned about their own. In this they are like us as well. Or, as Mr. Sitchin says, "I don't like to speak of them as aliens; they are too much like us."

Another matter on which the gods shed light is the orthodox concern with sin, original sin and eternal life.

The greatest high holy day of Judaism appears to be Yom Kippur, the day of atonement. On that day in the ancient rite the Kohan (Priest), by what appears to be a telepathic act, takes the sins from all the people and puts them on the scapegoat who is driven into the desert to be consumed by the demon Hazazel. This Hazazel is identified by the book of Noah as an Igigi, a watcher who came down against orders to enjoy human women. This act is shown to be the reason why God allowed human beings to be destroyed by the flood. It seems likely that this, not the actions of Eve, is the seed of the notion of Original Sin. If it is, the whole problem is a bad god. It seems also likely that Hazazel, whose name means lord of the flies, is the original model for the Christian (and Moslem) Devil.

The Fallen Angels

As supplemental reading one may refer to the Book of Enoch, a fascinating volume discovered in Ethiopia and written in Coptic. It is actually a lost book of the Bible that seems to have been dropped from the canon about 450 AD. Enoch is the Hebrew form of the Sumerian name ENMEDURANKI, king of Erech, to whom the ME are originally delivered. The Coptic book seems to give him a more Semitic character and the book is more or less an Old Testament version of the Apocalypse of St. John (Revelation). But to read it is to discover a remarkable thing: it contains a long extract from the book of Noah (a lost book of the Bible referred to in Genesis as part of its bibliography). More interesting still, the segment is a longer piece from which the "sons of God" (Nefilim) segment referred to earlier is taken.

The segment clearly explains the origin of Hazazel, the demon of Yom Kippur. It states that he is a watcher (Igigi) who is stationed "between heaven and earth" on what the Sumerians describe as an orbiting satellite. While there, he notices that human beings are enjoying each other sexually and decides to "come down" (against orders) to join in, a pleasure that seems to have been denied to him as part of a population control problem.

He therefore stops being an Igigi (Watcher) and becomes a Nefilim (One who comes down).

He brings some of his friends with him (The devil and his angels?). They descend on Mt. Hermon, and proceed to not only enjoy women, but to have children by them. From this, the general moral climate is so corrupted that the chief god (Enlil in Sumerian) decides to be rid of humans in general and so orders that human beings are not to be warned of an impending catastrophe set off by the return of Nibiru to the vicinity of Earth: the great flood. The Sumerians tell us that his brother Enki ruined his plans by telling Utnapishtim (Noah, Deucalion) that he should build a submarine (the Ark) and survive with his family and friends, and the "seed of many creatures."

Eternal Life

As for eternal life, it appears that the normal life span of a god is in the order of 300,000 earth years. That is not eternal, but it might seem so to us. Since we are half god, according to the Sumerian story of creation, we have a recessive gene for the 300,000 year life span.

The trees in the garden refer to Knowledge and Life. The knowledge is carnal knowledge, that we learn how to reproduce on our own; the life is 300,000 years — this become the quest for the holy grail and the substance of the promise of Jesus which seems to extend the life span indefinitely in an altered state.

These are matters dear to the heart of Western Orthodoxy. Instead of threatening these tenets the reality of the gods only strengthens their historical authenticity.

Government Orthodoxy

But what about the government? It could easily be predicted that the governmental orthodoxy would view the advent of the gods or the very existence of historical probability of such an advent, especially in the immediate future, with great alarm. This is what we might call the UFO aspect.

It should be noticed that the United States government and the French government take approaches to the subject that are almost diametrically opposed. The American government after the Roswell incident gave orders to suppress all the evidence. Since that time a lot of evidence has been suppressed. The French government, on the other hand, responded to the situation by establishing at the Cabinet level a department of UFOs.

Instead of suppressing the evidence they went all over the world seeking it and correlating it. In the seventies an article was published in *L'Express* (the French version of *Time*) written by the head of the department; I read it in French at the time. In essence he said that they have correlated numerous sightings, being very aware of the danger of fraud. The results were startling! The unequivocal nature of the beings and their equipment and mode of conduct from sources all over the world was very convincing.

Here is the summary: "We have determined from a correlation of the evidence and a consideration of its interrelationship that only two possibilities, or a combination of the two are possible: either we are being visited by beings from another system whose concern for our welfare passes our understanding, or there is an outbreak of the human unconscious as described by Carl Jung on a massive scale unprecedented in history. In either event it is the most significant event of the twentieth century."

The US government's apparent blind eye has a very reasonable explanation. They are afraid of culture shock. They are afraid the cities will burn if the matter is taken seriously. Such a response by people in the streets is not rational, but also very likely under certain circumstances.

There has been a change in public attitude, however, since the 1950s. The polls show that in the fifties some 30% of the people were able to accept the idea of "aliens." The latest poll shows 70%. Does that make it safe now? NASA announced evidence of life on Mars the other day. Does that signal a change in policy? Laurence Rockefeller would like to see a reversal of policy, and at one point was prepared to ask the president. Perhaps it is safe now, but even more important, perhaps it is not safe to continue the silence. A dramatic appearance could still have disastrous consequences for an unprepared public.

What Sitchin Has Done

How is Zecharia Sitchin involved? Very deeply. If the "others" do show up on Main Street it would be good to have an educated public who could look back on a long history of such contacts that proceeded with relative safety, and not to have a large segment of the public dreading the aliens of "Independence Day."

Mr. Sitchin went to the trouble of telling us in *Genesis Revisited* that he approached the Naval Observatory in Washington regarding the search for a new planet in our solar system. He was gratified to find that he was well received by an astronomer who had a copy of his book on the shelf behind him. In summary it appears that the Sumerian gods are with us, and that Zecharia Sitchin has proclaimed them.

It appears that these gods are deeply involved in our history as a race, but they have faded from human consciousness.

It appears that the reappearance of the gods in our consciousness is immanent if not already begun, and that to avoid the debilitating effects of culture shock we should consider seriously how to cope with these emergents and how our orthodoxy, whether scientific, religious, individual or governmental, will cope with them.

After I read Mr. Sitchin's first book, *The 12th Planet,* the following poem occurred to me after reading how the god Enki, man's friend, established the first city on a virgin Earth more than 400,000 years ago and called it ERIDU.

> Who art thou, Oh Eridu
> A buried city on a buried sea?
> Water borne
> Thy dust has lain
> Dreaming in the mist of time.
> But who hath waked thee Eridu?
> With memory of gods
> As familiar to us as ourselves
> As comfortable,
> And as mysterious.

(Eridu is 25 miles from Ur, the birthplace of Abraham, and has been excavated).

Scene: Southern Iraq.

Time: Yesterday, Today, and Tomorrow.

Marlene Evans earned her doctorate at Syracuse University in 1978 in the discipline of geography. She focused her early studies on environmental perception, human impacts on the Earth, persistent landscape features, as well as a study of various topics related to the variation in patterns of human occupance and livelihood around the globe. Her doctoral research drew on her undergraduate background in psychology and cartographic analysis, looking at the perceptual encounter with mapped information. Recently, her focus has turned to an exploration of ancient enigmatic landscapes in an effort to search out their meaning for early peoples, especially features like Newgrange in Ireland, and Stonehenge, Avebury and Silbury Hill in England. Dr. Evans holds the rank of professor at the State University of New York's Empire State College, where for twenty-three years she has taught and guided undergraduate and graduate adult learners pursuing degrees. Her teaching emphases include the social sciences and their methodologies, human impacts on the land, cultural patterns of occupance, future studies and earth science. She is a member of the International Association for New Science (IANS), the Association of American Geographers, the World Future Society, the Institute for Noetic Science, the Planetary Society, and numerous national environmental organizations, including the Adirondack Council.

Abstract

Discussion here argues that Zecharia Sitchin's work enlarges the available explanatory framework of human origins and history, supporting the argument that his work meets all the conditions necessary to formally acknowledge a *shift* in the human origins paradigm. The most provocative shift is from a body of explanation appropriately called the *"origins debate"* to another best described as the *"other terrestrial origins"* (OT) human origins paradigm. Using Sumerian tablet evidence Sitchin lays out the role of the Anunnaki (from the planet Nibiru) as the genetic designers of humans. How we initially react to this information and process it intellectually is explored in this discussion. Sitchin's more encompassing framework forces us to consider the future of human endeavors on this planet and the impending impact of the return of Nibiru. Discussion concludes by using a futures analytical framework to explore possible, probable, and preferable outcomes of the return of the Planet Nibiru and the Anunnaki to the vicinity of Earth in a near future time.

THE PARADIGM HAS SHIFTED: WHAT'S NEXT?

by

Marlene Evans, Ph.D.

That Zecharia Sitchin's work breaks new ground is an understatement. His seven books make a compelling case for the probability (meaning what likely will become known in the future) that intelligent sentient beings from a planet that belongs to our Solar System colonized Earth nearly 445,000 years ago. The Sumerian tablets provide the main body of evidence from which Sitchin carefully and prudently constructs a coherent explanation of the scientific endeavors and numerous exploits of the Anunnaki, who are, in essence, the technologically advanced interplanetary explorers who genetically engineered *homo sapiens sapiens.*

It becomes obvious to those who look seriously at Sitchin's work that his books, taken together, contain far reaching implications of such a profound nature that after a first encounter, even a skeptical reader is compelled to deal *in some way* with this information. Some come through their *Sitchin encounter* accepting his explanations. Others reject these explanations. Regardless of one's position, Sitchin's work serves as a trigger prompting us to consider *changing* our prior way of making meaning, and suggests we open our considerations to a much wider range of explanations. These potential changes in our thinking force us to reexamine what we have come to know from our educational background and what is set out in the traditional literature.

In Sitchin's material the topic of human origins is one of the most provocative contributions he offers us. In the encounter ex-

Copyright © Marlene Evans, 1996

perience, we find ourselves needing to build a different way of "making meaning" of this body of material, especially when we acknowledge the topic's implications. The array of possible implications suggested by Sitchin are more far reaching than the traditional explanations of how humans came to inhabit this planet.

The Sitchin *encounter reaction* generates an enlargement of our perspectives; we explore this reaction in this discussion, reviewing the most common reactions available to us — either *acceptance* or *rejection* of his information and interpretations. In place of a superficial assertion that Sitchin prompts a paradigm shift, we look closely at what happens to one's perspectives when one accepts Sitchin's evidence; in essence we examine *how* a paradigm shift occurs. We establish that, indeed, Sitchin's work prompts a paradigm shift. After this shift, curiosity prompts us to ask: What happens next? Then we explore the realm of possibilities and probabilities, unfolding some of the implications of Sitchin's material for our future.

The rejecting responses also receives attention. To better understand why some who encounter Sitchin's material develop a posture of rejection, "status quo" mindsets are reviewed. We find they are legitimated by the current realm of normal science, that body of explanations we have been given over our lifetimes. Why some hang on to this material and resist even a consideration of change is looked at. Finally, the existing "origins debate" versus Sitchin's "other terrestrial" explanation (called here the OT paradigm) is subjected to a futures analysis using consideration of the possible, probable, and preferable outcomes. Future scenarios and outcomes of the Sitchin material also are suggested.

Paradigms

The way we make meaning about the world around us involves drawing on a body of legitimated explanatory frameworks we have absorbed over the years. These all-encompassing explanations are known as *paradigms.* A *paradigm* serves as a framework we can use to draw conclusions, build generalizations, and under it, puzzles can be solved (in the scientific sense). In doing these things, paradigms contribute to a way of thinking about and understanding the world around us (Mohr, 1977).

Existing explanations have two primary characteristics, according to Thomas Kuhn (1962), who has made the most pervasive contribution to our understanding of paradigms and how they have brought about change in the history of science. In talking about the knowledge that establishes paradigms that already have become acceptable, Kuhn says, "first their achievement was sufficiently *unprecedented,* attracting an enduring group of adherents away from competing modes of scientific activity [and second], these achievements were sufficiently open-ended [so as] to leave all sorts of problems for the redefined group of adherents to attack" (1962, p. 10).

For a *new* paradigm to take hold, then, it must be provocative enough to be called unprecedented, it must attract a group of "believers" away from the existing explanations, and to do this, it must provide a wider scope of explanation. At the same time, this new material must be rational, coherent, and carefully grounded with data supporting it so that it is scientifically convincing, as well as factually verifiable. Further, a new paradigm is expected to meet the rest of conditions Kuhn lays out, meaning that it must hold considerable potential for responding to numerous unanswered questions, and at least intelligently attack and perhaps even solve several other observed puzzles. Let's see if Sitchin's work meets Kuhn's conditions.

Certainly, Sitchin's content is unprecedented. Look at the substance of his report: a bold and majestic 12th planet of the *Solar System of Apsu (the* Sumerian name for our Sun) is the home world of the sentient beings who first colonized Earth by coming to the planet using yet undiscovered (on Earth) space travel vehicles;

likely they built mega-earthworks on the planet's landscape for purposes we have not yet discovered; and eventually they genetically engineered the earthlings we today call humans. That beings from another planet (that only comes into Earth's vicinity every 3600 years because of its elliptical orbit) used genetic engineering to "blend" their genes with those of an existing hominid certainly is a "different" understanding of human origins. We have to admit that we recognize the plausibility of this explanation now that genetic engineering and our 20th century science has successfully created several "test tube" babies. That these Anunnaki OTs genetically engineered humans certainly was considered unbelievable to the early scholars who first uncovered and analyzed the tablets. However, the tablets stand as verifiable evidence, and those doubtful of the way Sitchin has interpreted this evidence have only to learn the ancient language systems and to walk in Sitchin's footsteps, reading the tablets for themselves.

Careful inspection of Sitchin's explanation of human origins reveals the scope of this topic to be considerably wider now than with the existing explanations we had available pre-Sitchin. As to large groups of adherents, we find acceptance of Sitchin's work growing in the global public arena. His work is accepted and is circulating widely (as measured by where and how many people have purchased his books); he now has published seven books in 14 languages, and millions of copies have been sold around the world. That resistance to Sitchin's work arises in the traditional scholarly circles is not unexplainable. Sitchin would not be the first scholar to break new ground and to be rejected by the establishment. We all remember the most famous case — that of Galileo.

Moreover, Sitchin's explanations answer numerous questions that have gone unanswered for a very long time, and provoke also several new questions. For example, the role of the Anunnaki in human history suggests explanations for several enigmatic phenomena that have defied explanation and stumped scholars for centuries, like when the Sphinx was built (which relates to who built it), and what purposes Stonehenge and Newgrange served thousands of years ago, just to mention some of the most well known enigmatic phenomena. Without going further with more detail, we easily can see that the Sitchin material does indeed present a *different* paradigm for explaining the origins of human-kind from the ones we typically have learned about. The question now is: so what?

When we look at existing explanations of human origins, we find two of these explanations form a raging debate. Each takes an irreconcilable position against the other; here we will call these discussions the *"origins debate."* In this debate, human *evolution* as given by the traditional scientific explanation is *pitted against* a more religiously structured argument that falls under the label of *creationism.* Sitchin's explanations justifiably can be seen as a trigger shifting perspectives *away* from this "debate" paradigm. When we use the exegesis provided by Zecharia Sitchin as the backdrop for discussion, we find a highly provocative message indeed. If it were science fiction, we could dismiss it. But it is not. Instead, it is something quite different; it is a well-reasoned, rational, and factually grounded explanation from the tangible scientific (clay tablet) evidence that OTs genetically engineered humans. In fact, using perspectives suggested by Sitchin, we probably should call this alternative explanation for human origins the *"other terrestrial origins"* paradigm, instead of referring to beings from "other worlds" by the more commonly used label — ETs.

It is not our intent here to delve into either of the debate positions, only to point out that this debate continues and seems irreconcilable, causing an ever widening rift between the two sides. With Sitchin's work in hand, we can see that the focus of the entire discussion about how humans came into being *steps beyond* traditional discussion, enlarging it and encompassing both the positions of the evolutionists and the creationists. Thoughtful consideration of *all* this evidence suggests Sitchin's material could serve as a possible bridge for resolution of the debate. Important to any possible reconciliation of the traditional origins debate is recognition of where this enlarged viewpoint obtains its authority.

Sitchin's base of authority, the tablets, were scribed nearly three millennia *before the Bible*, which is the source which creationists use to ground their argument. Interestingly, Sitchin points out that the tablets illuminate the stories in Genesis by expanding them. Sitchin's cogent discussion of the creation account (in Chapter 12 of his book, *The l2th Planet)* suggests a congruence between the tablet data and the *Bible's* more compressed presentation, which came millennia later. The important point here is *not* how the tablets came to underpin the Bible's Genesis accounts, but that in place of the contesting and irreconcilable viewpoints now informing the *either-or* arguments of the debate paradigm, stands a new viewpoint. In fact this discussion argues for replacement of the entire origins debate with the *other terrestrial origins* (OT) paradigm suggested by Sitchin's work.

The Sitchin Encounter

What a reader of any of Zecharia Sitchin's books clearly realizes is that Sitchin is an explorer. How do we know this? Look at the evidence. First, he is bold, brave and undaunted. He ventures into what most of us would call a "no man's land" (which contains the realm of ancient clay tablets scribed in cuneiform language), where he reads and re-interprets their messages and maps out his findings on the factual and conceptual landscape; and finally, he reports (in published form) to his arm chair audience. This is what explorers do. Interestingly, Sitchin readers cannot passively glide through the pages of his carefully crafted discussions without realizing his books contain new information. Having encountered it, we are obliged to ask: what does one *do* with this new information?

First, we must confront the fact that the substance of Sitchin's material lies outside and beyond our already developed understandings of human origins and history, and this realization catapults us into personally uncharted territory. While Sitchin's explorations cut a wide swath across several jungles on the conceptual landscape, it is *we* the readers who do the discovering on this expedition. With each new chapter, we are enlightened, and moved, subtly but irreversibly, into another world of understanding, into discovering another reality, one ripe with implications for our future. And this other reality is made plausible by the facts scribed in clay.

In addition, *something else* happens when we read this material. Sitchin's explications of the ancient data bring us face to face with our own personal frontier of knowledge. In fact, we are forced to confront our world view in an "up close and personal" way when we encounter Sitchin because it shakes up everything we have learned previously. It is the strength and structure of our world view that is brought into question by this material, and our world view comes squarely into play because it is constructed by what we know, and *it* determines whether we either accept or reject new information, especially information that calls into question what we know about the origins of the human race.

Careful inspection of what we know — and believe — reveals that in the encounter with Sitchin's work, our world view comes under attack. When we try to bolster ourselves against this attack, we are forced to read more deeply into Sitchin, and what happens then is that we find ourselves sucked "over the line," taken beyond our personal intellectual frontier — an intellectual process that thrusts us into our personal "no-man's land." For most of us, whether or not to cross this frontier was *not* an available choice. We are propelled by the logic and scope of Sitchin's scholarship into the other reality his material creates, a reality that represents a distinctly different way of explaining history than we have ever read about or heard of previously. After our Sitchin encounter we are left wondering what happened to us. Our mind generates a cascade of questions. Why have we not heard about this before? Where is all this coming from? *Is this stuff true?* What does this mean?

Later in this chapter, some selected implications about future implications will be explored. But first, let us deal here with the question of the validity of Sitchin's story. To contest the validity of Sitchin's discussions, one would need to go directly to the original materials, reading and interpreting the Sumerian tablets as he did. Obvious limitations force us to take another approach, one that focuses more closely on the work itself. Even a cursory reading shows us that Sitchin carefully grounds his discussion on original sources (even more were included in the first book before the commercial process edited them out) that build conscientiously on the early scholarship developed after these tablets were discovered. Sitchin also worked with the original published reports of notable archaeologists who first uncovered the tablets and performed the linguistic redaction, including such recognizable scholars as George Smith (1876), Leonard W. King (1902), and Stephen Langdon (1909), all who wrote about the redacted texts for the first time.

However, Sitchin's interpretations are different. They must be — he is working in a technologically different context. In fact, his work differs from those original archaeological writings in two key ways. First, he did not do the archaeological excavations. He did not dig up the tablets and say, "Look what I found. This is what these tablets say." Second, he read the original data with the perspectives and insight of a late 20th century man, then cast a modern space-age context around these messages laid down on the tablets thousands of years ago. The context in which Smith, King and Langdon wrote (at the end of the 19th and first part of the 20th centuries) did not have the benefit of the technology we now consider commonplace. Then, no understanding existed of flying machines, or more importantly, of rocketing men to the Moon, of a powerful telescope that could be launched for reconnaissance into deep space, of interplanetary reconnaissance technology capable of photographing other planets, or even of a theoretical ability to send people to Mars. To account for the differences between Sitchin's work and that of the early scholars we find that *they were born too soon* to have the benefit of our recently developed space exploration technology to use as a context for their interpretation of the artifacts.

The Encounter Reaction

The implications of the Sitchin discussions are more than challenging — they are mind-boggling and even astounding, primarily because we have not heard of this body of explanation before. In a nutshell, the message is provocative: more than 445,000 years ago a small group of sentient beings came to this planet and, among other endeavors, genetically engineered earthlings. When we process the inherent implications of just this small portion of the Sitchin message, we find ourselves faced with a choice. We either can accept his discussion, *or* we can reject the information altogether.

Several possible reasons to account for a rejection stance come to mind. Rejection would suggest that we recognize our personal world view is inadequate. Abject denial of the validity of the information could mean that this entire body of ideas represents a serious threat to one's existing belief system. That prompts a wall of emotional rejection to come up. If we consider ourselves even fairly well-educated, or more importantly, if our personal expertise is touched on by this new material, and if the implications of Sitchin's material would overturn our established knowledge base, we have to face a serious threat to our ego. We find ourselves saying: "Wait a minute. My expertise is in jeopardy! If I accept this stuff, I'll have to completely reorganize what I have learned!" Likely our ego "pipes up" to defend itself, calling the author of this new information a "fraud," or worse yet, a "heretic."

Our world view is built across our lifetime, resulting from enormous study efforts, and this world view gives us our sense of security. It operates like attitudes, clinging like transparent shrink-wrap to deeper constructs in our reservoirs of attitude and knowledge. In these deep spaces, we also store our values and beliefs. All this "stuff" is what we call *our knowledge*. Our individual world view is the container for all this knowledge. We strengthen the walls of our world view through hard intellectual work, and like any protective structure, it represents something we can hide within when the winds of change blow hard. In other words, it is our base of security. So, when our world view is challenged by information that takes us "beyond our experience," many fight back with a denial reaction. We want to deny both the validity of the information that generates the threat, and we want to devalue the importance of all that "new stuff" that makes us feel so insecure. We find ourselves saying, "No, no, no! It can't possibly be like that!"

When we look closely at what props up our world view, we find, in actuality, it is our *sense of self.* New perspectives and information must be integrated into our existing explanation of who we are (our self concept). Our sense of self defines our inner meanings of our identity. Because our self concept organizes and constricts our reality, the implication here is clear — when we encounter new information we have to integrate it into our self concept. To tinker with our sense of self is dangerous work! Our personal world view organizes and constricts, thereby giving shape and boundary to what we are willing to see and learn about the world. To accept new, previously unheard of information means we need to re-organize *all* that material already in place, and that is a huge undertaking. It doesn't take much to realize the scope of the rethinking and readjustment one needs to do — or the nature of the threat that forces a rejection stance. The public at large seems to have less trouble engaging his material than does the community of scholars who, supposedly, are committed to advancing the boundaries of knowledge. There is little we can do with those who adopt a denial stance, except wait until the new explanatory paradigm is so well established they have little ground left on which to attach their denial.

In retrospect, when we think back to how we "felt" after first reading the Sitchin materials, we find some interesting insights. We had to decide whether what were reading was truth, or not. Our feelings, in fact, probably were tinged with doubt. What we began to realize, if we stayed with these feelings, was a *shift* in our way of making meaning about human origins was in motion. We first had to recognize that what we were reading was a completely different body of knowledge than we had ever heard of before. Then, we began to "toggle back and forth" between thinking, "Wow, this is fantastic! But, wait a minute, it can't be true. But look at the evidence this guy brings forward. Wow! Maybe it *is* true. Even if it is true, what does all this mean?"

In fact, one's entire way of thinking likely was enlarging when we began to really "process" the results of this encounter. What likely took time, though, after we recovered from this mind-blowing awareness, was that we now needed to restructure our background meanings. We had to rebuild our world view. Cataloguing all of the types of knowledge that needed adjusting, and drawing the linkages between the new and the old perspectives constituted the intellectual work we did indeed undertake if we came through this experience accepting the Sitchin material positively.

The Shifted Paradigm

Let us now look carefully at the types of things that happen when a paradigm shifts. First, the interpretations that can be made from a reassessment of the old facts are enlarged, which means that the entire explanatory framework expands. Clearly, the revolution is on its way when a "gestalt switch" or a "conversion" occurs in the way of thinking of even a small group who seriously engage the material. When this kind of a shift occurs, according to Casti (1989), *everything* related to the old construct is reexamined and most likely needs to be transformed. When the shift in the paradigm begins, no order exists — only chaos reigns. In the beginning, logic typically has little to do with seeing and accepting the new paradigm. *Recognizing* a shift in the prevailing paradigm is not a matter of calling on logic. In fact, logic seems to abandon us. Acceptance isn't even an arguable matter. Argument would require one's logical and rational capabilities to be in good order. Instead, we must draw on our "gut feelings."

Making a serious shift in one's intellectual habits of thinking is a rare event, in that seldom have we had to even think about doing this. But, shifting a paradigm is *not* a new experience in the history of scientific thought. One historian of science, John Casti (1989), characterizes such a *change* in our way of seeing like this: We make meaning and interpret information by using a pair of conceptual glasses through which we typically see and engage the world and solve its puzzles — called the normal science realm — and suddenly, our glasses are smashed. When we put on a new pair, what — and how — we see is quite different. This new view is the *shifted paradigm.*

As a result of the impact of the Sitchin material, a radical change of perspective does indeed take over in our mind. His work pushes all of the contemporary explanations back into the normal science explanatory realm and allows us to see beyond our personal frontier. His careful, scholarly reinterpretation of the ancient evidence catapults us into an "other world" realm where we find ourselves lonely among our colleagues. In short, Sitchin has generated what Thomas Kuhn's enormously influential book describes as a *"scientific revolution."*

Mounting any challenge to the existing body of normal science holds potential for weakening the existing paradigms. Kuhn (1962) lays the blame for a weakened old paradigm on an accumulation of anomalies — observations or explanations that used to appear to fit under the old explanatory framework, but no longer do, or for which the old explanations are inadequate or even incorrect. The old explanatory framework is in serious trouble when an ever growing body of observations becomes enigmatic, and the sharp thinkers among us suddenly become converts. Almost immediately, these converts seem to lose their confidence in the traditional ideas provided by the well worn explanations, especially after they see the scope of the new explanation, and check the validity of the data that underpins what can be called the new paradigm. Chalmers (1976) goes further by indicating that a weakening of the existing paradigm occurs when heretical ideas are even allowed into the discussion.

As social beings, we do not live outside the normal science paradigms. These are the operating paradigms that comprise normal science and guide our learning processes. According to one practicing scientist whose work is strongly philosophical, Hans Mohr (1977), operating paradigms include a certain line of thinking, or even a culture of thought. They shape what we believe to be "the way it is," scientist and layman alike. Supposedly, new ideas are encouraged in the realm of normal science. However, although we are taught that it is the role of normal science to question the existing paradigms, to test theories, to construct new models, and with reputable evidence, to offer better, richer, more complete explanations, *paradoxically,* the really good ideas are treated disdainfully when first set out.

Mohr offers us a revealing glimpse into the somewhat contradictory behavior that exists in the domain of normal science. He confesses that anyone making even a minor step outside the existing paradigm can encounter "strong and embittered reluctance" (1977, p. 130). Kuhn (1962) gives a much stronger interpretation of the consequences of daring to challenge, redefine, or even just expand the existing body of knowledge. He points out that when scientific revolutions occur they involve intellectual rather than liquid bloodshed of a similar order of magnitude to that found in the political arena.

As scientists of humankind, then, we appreciate and respect the normal science paradigms that illuminate the material and biological worlds, because these paradigms represent an enormous body of hard-won knowledge that is acquired through considerable personal sacrifice. We truly *earn* our stripes in this arena. This is why we think long and hard before "grabbing" onto a very different explanation. Traditional ways of thinking are the realm of normal scientists; in this realm we hold mindsets which are rooted firmly in their accumulated knowledge — it truly is an investment.

How, then, do new ideas, grounded provable ideas, those that coalesce the largest array of facts and recast old explanations in a more comprehensive model ever get to see the light of day? And, when they do, how do they survive? The answer is clear: the authors of such bold and overarching ideas must be — and are — personally steadfast and factually confident, and their proponents must be prepared to assist in carrying forward a seemingly unacceptable message. So, it is the creativity of the proponents that must persevere in perfecting the message. What they must do, speaking "mental-physically," is put the old wine in new bottles and completely re-label it.

If we pause for just a moment to ask "How did Sitchin come to catch on to these new ideas, embedded as they were in the old paradigm?" One possible explanation comes to the surface. A distinguishing feature of the very early scholarship is that when these archaeologists and linguists could not understand the nature of the text they were reading, or recognize the content, they decided they were reading *myth*. Sitchin, on the other hand, takes the view that the tablets represent *actual history*. So, he didn't let go of the enigmatic parts of the tablet stories until he figured out what the texts *could actually* mean. With the late 20th century context in his head, along with his careful and thorough approach to scholarship, he did just that — figured out a set of plausible meanings. This is *how* Sitchin shifted the paradigm.

For those of us who would like to further the shifted paradigm, we must learn to recognize those mindsets in abject denial to the Sitchin ideas, and we must distinguish them from those whose minds are receptive. When facing entrenched habitual mindsets, an awareness of the tenacity of the "old" way of thinking must be brought "front and center." We must acknowledge that new ways of thinking are not easy to develop. Nothing can be done to "convince" an individual who holds beliefs that are tightly wrapped in emotion. But, we also recognize that an ability to engage in "new think" is essential in promoting a new paradigm. How to recognize those who are potentially receptive is essential for anyone trying to encourage the spread of the core ideas needed to promulgate a paradigm shift. This information is offered to increase the reader's insight and awareness of when to push forward and when to back off.

Future Implications

After the paradigm shifts — then what? What are the implications of this different explanation — this enlarged viewpoint set out by Zecharia Sitchin? Equally or even more importantly: What does the Sitchin material mean for our personal futures? Certainly the future implications of the Sitchin material need to be identified and explored. But, how do we do that? We can't *see into* the future, so how can we even begin to discuss future impacts logically, or scientifically? Furthermore, how can we get at implications that will unfold only through the passage of future time?

Discussion now turns to consider these questions. These are not new questions for students of future studies, a field that has an identifiable methodology and has attracted considerable scholarship. Before we delve briefly into the futures approach, we first must assume that we all now have accepted the Sitchin material as a sound, plausible analysis of what the tablets say in 20th (or even 21st) century terms. Without acceptance of this assumption, no discussion of future outcomes is meaningful.

In actuality, futures are an extension of our present conceptualizations on a time line that begins with what we call "history" and supposedly moves in a linear manner to that realm we have learned to call "the future." Historical material is valued for its role in setting trends in motion and providing us a body of potentialities. While a futures methodology works with the "right-hand" end of the timeline, it does not ignore the full time line. Interestingly, the idea of parallel universes, as set out by Fred Alan Wolf (1988), might force us to redefine the concept of a "time line."

A distinguished futurist, Edwin Cornish (1977), indicates that futurists have a unique perspective on the world. In his view, a futures perspective consists of and builds on three underlying assumptions. The first is that futurists assume there exists a *unity of reality,* and this unity is interconnected across time. You can't "time warp" into a viable future. Just as you have to move through Mach 1 to get to Mach 2, you move in a connected way through time. Second, futurists assume that *time* serves as a crucial factor for energizing the change trajectory. Futurists believe that the thought forms provide a distinctly different way of defining events — we "design" our futures — they don't just happen. Third, it is assumed that *ideas* focused on the future form the basis of legitimate and viable conceptualizations. Ideas are considered *futurables,* in the commodity sense, and are the "tools of thought" of the futures trade. However, for futurists, no ready formulas for "foreseeing" consequences are used to project outcomes. Futures is *not* prediction; it is rational projected conceptualization.

Using a futures perspective for analysis forces us to look at the information in hand to identify trends in motion, and to carefully identify and consider arrays of outcomes that cover several different ways of approaching the time line. These likely outcomes serve to open consideration of likely consequences, and thus can be organized under a three-part model that allows a *way of conceptualizing* future outcomes. This type of consideration covers *possible, probable* and *preferable* outcomes. These dimensions set out a way of conceptualizing three associated types of futures: what *could* be, what *might* be, and what *should* be (Henchy, 1977).

Before we look squarely at the future implications of the Sitchin work, and to illustrate how the futures methodology works, we first will look at the key argument that structured an early portion of this chapter, the "origins debate." This debate is identified as the normal science position "pre-Sitchin." We can subject the structure of this debate — meaning the two positions — to a futures analysis using the possible, probable and preferable outcomes framework. Keep in mind: *Possible* outcomes allow us to look at the range of options — this comprises the first step in the analysis. *Probable* outcomes allow us to examine each possible outcome identified for their probability of occurrence. *Preferable* outcomes give us permission to weave in personal and societal preferences. Preferable outcomes consist of what we would *like to* see occur, given the unfoldment of selected units of time. This brings into play personal free-will choice and allows us to consider its role and influence in making a selection of outcomes we are willing to accept. This is akin to making the selection of which path we would *like to* walk on to get to a destination, and picking the one that would allow us to see the type of scenery (outcome) we value most. Choices include outcomes that would be: enlightening, satisfying, beneficial, educational, palatable, tolerable or even disdainful.

Let us lay out the *possible future* options available under the debate paradigm. We could expect the origins debate will continue, with both evolutionists and creationists holding firm to their positions, thus maintaining the "status quo" (possible future 1). Another option open for consideration is that one side in this debate — either one — will acknowledge the enlarged viewpoint set out by Sitchin, and the debate itself will collapse for lack of opposition (possible future 2). The third possibility is that both sides will "shift" to acknowledge the wisdom that is inherent in the Sitchin position (possible future 3).

Considering *probable future outcomes* allows us to assess the probability of each of the range of possibilities identified in step one. The strongest approach to determine probabilities is one using a mathematical formula. Considering the three possibilities outlined above, a probability of one-third ($p = 0.333$) can be assigned to each possible (projected) outcome. The decimal number used above must total the integer one ($p = 1.0$) and is assigned under the assumption that each of the three possibilities has an *equal* chance of selection. However, because of the underlying assumption of the interconnectedness of reality, we must acknowledge the contextual circumstances in which these possibilities exist. Another influencing factor in futurizing, deals with acknowledging trends in motion.

A confounding factor impinging on our ability to work with confidence with equal probabilities as identified above is the societal context within which these probabilities operate. In the case of the origins debate, each side believes in the rationality and immutability of their position. It is the nature and source of the evidence used by each side in the debate that in actuality is under contention. Faith is at the root of one position, and scientifically identified factual evidence underpins the other. When examined closely, these two approaches *cannot* be reconciled on the merits of the evidence used to structure each argument. Faith is emotionally defined (meaning it defies rational argument), and either leads to full acceptance or full rejection of any position. Factual evidence is embraced as important to the scientific side, provided it was selected and analyzed under the terms of the scientific method, meaning it used rigorous sampling, it employed recognizable and repeatable methods of data analysis, and precautions were taken in the implementation of the methodology to prevent bias and preserve objectivity. With no common ground on which to base discourse, these positions are irreconcilable.

How can we discuss the concept of change of the "origins debate?" One possible solution is offered by Kuhn, who tells us that existing (normal science) paradigms "die out," essentially implying that their proponents *never* change their minds, they just are eliminated through time. New intellectual positions are taught to the young before these "fresh receptive minds" have a chance to become traditional *mindsets*. This discussion can move no further, only time can unfold these outcomes. While this last statement appears as a "cop out," there are few other viable alternatives — unless the realm of parallel universes is introduced. To pursue the possible outcomes inherent in this topic would deflect this discussion, and is given no further attention here.

However, there is a structural irony associated with the idea of "teaching" scientific reasoning to adherents of the creationist side of the origins debate. In rejecting the evolutionist position, many currently defining this view reject the role and objective of scientific thinking. In doing so, they sweep aside not only the evidence used in support of the evolutionist position, but all uses of the scientific method. The educational arena is the playing field of this consequence, and millions of children are being raised devoid of not only an appreciation of the role of science, but an inability to use it to solve everyday dilemmas.

Preferable futures introduce individual personal choices in defining outcomes. Each of us must define the preferable outcomes that illuminate our own values. If this writer were the "designer" of the futures options of the origins debate, deflation and elimination of the origins debate altogether would be the preferable future option. This would be accomplished by disseminating a wide array of evidence that would overturn and reorganize (not destroy) the literalist's interpretation of the *Bible*. It would see much of the Pseudepigrapha, original books not selected for inclusion in the *Bible* as we have come to know it, returned to widespread circulation. Much of this information also will illuminate what has come to be called biblical wisdom. Although most rational thinkers who have access to the information in the Sumerian tablets can see the parallels that exist between these ancient sources and the condensed summaries included in the Bible (which also were heavily edited during early church history), literalists probably will not alter their mindset in our lifetime as to what is "inspired text" and what is myth. Such is the nature of cultural tradition. The beauty of the Sitchin body of evidence on the origins debate is that it, in effect, walks away from the disputes identified in the debate.

Will the Anunnaki Return?

The futures approach applied to the debate paradigm now can be focused on selected topics covered in the Sitchin materials. The three-part futures model (used in the preceding section) will assist in the search for possible, probable and preferable futures outcomes. Because Sitchin's material covers a wide range of topics, the issues related to the return of the Anunnaki are the only topic selected for analysis here. To facilitate this discussion, the futures analytic model will *integrate* discussion of the possible, probable and preferable futures embedded in these questions: *Will the Anunnaki return? If so, when?*

To launch any discussion about whether the Anunnaki will return, first we must review some important historical evidence about the consequences of previous returns of Nibiru to our solar system. The *Epic of Creation* tablets set out a body of evidence explaining not only the existence of the Planet Nibiru, but how it shaped the formative history of Planet Earth. Accepting the Sitchin re-interpretations of those tablets allows us also to understand the consequences of Nibiru's return. Tablet evidence indicates that during one of Nibiru's orbits, the ice sheet on the Antarctic continent was destabilized (probably because of increased tectonic activity). It slipped into the surrounding oceans, creating a monumental tidal wave known as the Deluge or great flood. Most culture realms around the globe have a flood myth, which when taken together with the tablet evidence, establishes the validity of this event. The cause of the Deluge explained by Sitchin is the best, most logical explanation this writer has encountered of the cause of the Deluge.

Sitchin also discusses increased tectonic activity as a characteristic of Nibiru's return visit. Increased tectonic activity and its global effects is a *possible* future outcome deserving consideration. It would result from the adjustive instability of Earth's crust, which results from the circumstances created when Earth was formed. The tablets tell us that originally a planet which orbited between Jupiter and Mars, the ancient planet Tiamat, was struck by one of Nibiru's moons, and it broke into two parts. That part which became Earth was shunted into orbit in the position third from the Sun where we "reside" today.

During Nibiru's retrograde pass between Jupiter and Mars on its journey around our Sun, if Nibiru's mass is as large as it is projected to be (3-5 times larger than Earth), it would likely generate considerable gravitational effects on Earth's surface plates. Corroborating evidence (though not discussed in the Sitchin context) for increased plate tectonic "stresses" substantiating this *possible* future scenario can be implied from discussions set out by astronomer John Gribbin (1977) who has given some thought to causes of increased tectonic activity. Gribbin, former editor of the prestigious British journal, *Nature,* postulated excessive gravitational "pull" as a potential cause of serious tectonic activity as a result of periodic planetary alignment, which if involving at least three major planets, could generate serious plate movement and readjustments. This effect would be especially *plausible* if Earth, in its orbital year, during Nibiru's transit, was positioned on the "outer side" of the Sun in unobstructed proximity to the transit orbit of Nibiru. However, if Earth's orbital position was protected by the Sun, meaning it was on the "inner side" during Nibiru's solar pass, the tectonic effects would be attenuated. It is the fragile nature of the tectonic plates resulting from the formative destabilization of the planetary body that makes Earth's surface so vulnerable to such disruptional stresses, and therefore supports these scenarios.

The Sumerian tablets indicate the Anunnaki arrived on Planet Earth 445,000 years ago, and the return of the Planet Nibiru to the vicinity of the realm of our Sun, follows a periodicity of 3600 years. This would bring Nibiru into sufficient proximity before and after the actual "swipe" of this planet around the Sun, making the Anunnaki return to Earth a *possible* and *probable* event. Nibiru has not returned recently, meaning for at least the past three — or more — millennia, if one type of evidence of this return is *widespread* tectonic activity. If Nibiru *does* generate multiple events such as earthquakes, volcanic eruptions, tidal waves, and subduction of portions of the Earth's surface material, perhaps there is a linkage between the prophesied tectonic events and the return of Nibiru. This is a *possible* future to be considered. These data also support a *probable* future scenario.

An interesting body of material has been placed in the public arena that we can consider in support of these *possible* future scenarios. The second of two programs focusing on a convergence of prophecy was presented during the Fall of 1995 on NBC television. It indicates that the time frame for increased globally extensive tectonic activity will be between 1997 and 2012. The futuremost time corresponds with the end of the Mayan calendar. The near time is defined by various types of sources, including prophecies of the Hopi, Nostradamus, and other prophetic (psychic) sources. All these prophecies discuss Earth suffering serious tectonic effects.

It is interesting to note that return of the planet Nibiru and return of the Anunnaki are not necessarily synonymous. Sitchin is clear (in his in-person presentations) on this point. He bases his position on hard archaeological evidence. This evidence indicates that the Anunnaki were able to make the journey to Earth when Nibiru was in approach, but still a considerable distance away from our solar system, perhaps even still beyond the system's outer limits. In his book, *The 12th Planet,* Sitchin discusses artifact evidence in the form of a circular plaque which was carefully analyzed in 1912 and again in 1915 by Ernst Weidner. This disc, when subjected to the Sitchin analysis, indicates that the Anunnaki had a formula directing their flight pattern through the outer planets, and they had it scribed as a *route map* on a circular tablet. This artifact would support a highly *possible* scenario in support of the fact that the Anunnaki came from Nibiru *before* it arrived near its orbital position between Jupiter and Mars, and no doubt also *after* their planet's pass around our Sun. This evidence lends further support to the scenario outlining the return of the Anunnaki as a *possible and probable* future.

The answer to the question, *will* the Anunnaki return is: yes! Before we explore the "when" possibility, let us first raise the question of "if." Will the Anunnaki want to return to Earth? Historical evidence again gives us some clues to use in discussing this *possible* future. Their reason for inhabiting Earth (given in the tablet data) was to mine gold. Gold is still found on Earth, though perhaps it is not as plentiful as it was in the pre-earthling period. It might at first glance appear to be not so easily accessed at this point in the planet's history because gold resources are now under the jurisdiction of national entities who claim ownership of them. However, if the Anunnaki still need gold from this planet, they would only need to depose the earthlings who presume ownership of the deposit locations. One observation should be made clear. If the Anunnaki want this gold, they will have it! Human resistance would be futile. No technology exists on Earth — yet — that can defend against OT technology, which likely far exceeds anything we have or are likely to develop without OT assistance.

But there are other reasons the Anunnaki might want to return to Earth. It perhaps sounds a bit far-fetched and unreal, but it does constitute a *possible* scenario, supported with evidence. It is the "ant farm" scenario. It is possible that a technologically advanced civilization who were instrumental in "seeding" a planet with beings (especially beings who carry the same intellectual and spiritual qualities of their "creators"), might be *curious* about how these beings have learned to behave, what they have done with the endowments bequeathed to them, and how they have developed in spiritual ways. They might have the same scientific curiosity that we unleash on ants, bees, primates and any number of other forms of life we study. A *possible* scenario involves the Anunnaki return to see what we have done with ourselves. They will be dismayed with how overpopulated we have allowed the planet to become, and also how we have despoiled it.

The projected time frame of Nibiru's next return is not addressed in Sitchin's materials. However, there are some recent events in planetary science that are being called "harbingers" of Nibiru. The most noteworthy is the sighting of a celestial object (called at the time of this writing a comet). This comet is far brighter than would be expected at the distance it now is observed to be. Its magnitude appears larger (from estimates made during 1996) and its luminescence is brighter than is typical of most comets. Nevertheless, this object (called Hale-Bopp in honor of the two amateur astronomers who first sighted it) seems to have an elliptical orbit similar to that which the tablets indicate was characteristic of Nibiru (inclined 30 degrees below the ecliptic or plane of orbit of all planets in our solar system). This information allows us to build a strong investment in the *possibility* of a return of Nibiru in a time frame encompassing *most readers' lifetimes*. The unfolding of the future time line will provide the final support for these future scenarios. However, we must again be reminded that prediction is *not* the realm of scholarly future studies. It goes without saying, that to believe history is to be forewarned. The evidence reviewed here is a *possible* future scenario.

Discussion to this point deals primarily with geologic consequences. Now we turn toward evidence that represents promises by specific Anunnaki to earthlings (their term for humans). The Anunnaki, especially under Enki, were benevolent toward humankind. Sitchin's discussion indicates it was Enki who warned Noah of the pending Deluge, and thus was instrumental in saving humankind from *total* extinction. It is *possible* this attitude of benevolence still exists, and that a return would be positive, peaceful, and as productive as Sitchin indicates past "visits" have been. However, this same flood event was not positive for the majority of earthlings who existed at that time. The Sitchin discussion explains that it was out-of-control procreation that brought the flood's dire consequences to earthlings during the pre-flood period, and the flood was the result of Enlil's decision to wipe out the burgeoning population. It was Enlil who kept the impending flood information from humans and caused their demise, primarily because he could no longer tolerate the noise of the hordes. However, it also was Enlil who promised Noah on Mount Ararat after the vessel landed and was discovered (by Enlil), that no similar catastrophe would ensue again. In a return scenario, it is *possible* this promise still holds.

With Sitchin material as our beacon, we can see these several — and likely numerous other — possible and probable futures put out for discussion. We also can realize that *history,* as we have learned it from Sitchin's scholarship, defines these futures available to us. While all of the scenarios posed here are not wholly positive ones, it is this writer's belief that *we do indeed design* our futures. We must use what we know and have learned to build new ways of thinking and to alert humankind to potential directions of change, and in doing so, allow ourselves to select the most beneficial and enriching outcomes. Indeed, tectonic change would not be "kind" to all of humanity, but long-term survival of humans on this planet never has been totally benevolent. Yes, there are those individuals among us who would only select future scenarios that were financially and personally enriching. Greed will only be eliminated when focus on the material realm is dissipated.

There are those who are conceptually incapable of futurizing, or who want human energy focused *only* on earthly problems. This represents an Earth-centric viewpoint and ignores the reality that we are *not* alone in the Universe. However, the most productive scenarios, the *preferable* ones, are positive because they do not involve fear, an emotion that immobilizes our thoughts and slows our creative energies. Those that discuss "gloom and doom" outcomes do little to encourage positive mental energy useful in developing enlightening possible and plausible outcomes that would move mankind forward toward becoming a more humane, spiritual and intelligent species. Those scenarios that meet these progressively positive goals are the preferable ones.

This treatise concludes with a call to readers to continue what has only been set in motion as an initial step here. We began by asking: after the paradigm shifts, then what? We have established that the shift has occurred, and Sitchin is responsible. The possible, probable and preferable futures are the "gold" yet to be discovered and crafted into usable mental tools for the positive use of humankind. To your future efforts, we wish you "good luck." Write when you have possibles that are probable and positively preferable.

Make it so!

Acknowledgments

The author wishes to extend thanks to Michael Knapp, of Corinth, New York, a keen reader of Sitchin's books and one who understands the futures mindset, who patiently reviewed several drafts of this material and made numerous helpful suggestions. Also, it is only because of the interest and continued encouragement of Zecharia Sitchin that this discussion has "seen the light of day." To both, your assistance is most warmly appreciated.

REFERENCES

Casti, John. 1989. *Paradigms Lost — Images of Man in the Mirror of Science*. New York: William Morrow.

Chalmers, Alan. 1976. *What is This Thing Called Science?* St. Lucia: University of Queensland.

Cornish, Edwin. 1977. "Toward a Philosophy of Futurism," *The Futurist*, Vol. 11 (6), pp. 380-81.

Eicher, David. "Here Comes Hale-Bopp" *Astronomy,* Vol. 24 (2), pp. 68-73.

Gribbin, John. 1977. *Our Changing Planet*. New York: Crowell.

Gribbin, John and Stephen Plagemann. 1982. *The Jupiter Effect Reconsidered*. New York: Random House.

Henchy, Norman. 1977. "Building a Framework for the Study of the Future," *World Future Society Bulletin,* Vol. 11 (5), pp. 1-9

King, Leonard W. (1902). *The Seven Tablets of Creation* Vol. 1. London: Luzac.

Kuhn, Thomas. 1962. *The Structure of Scientific Revolutions*. Chicago: University of Chicago Press.

Langdon, Stephen. 1923. *The Babylonian Epic of Creation: Restored from the recently recovered Tablets of Assur*. Oxford, Clarendon.

Margolis, Howard. 1993. *Paradigms and Barriers — How Habits of Mind Govern Scientific Beliefs*. Chicago: University of Chicago.

Mohr, Hans. 1977. *Lectures on Structure and Significance of Science*. New York: Springer-Verlag.

Sitchin, Zecharia. 1976. *The 12th Planet*. Briarcliff Manner: Stein & Day.

Sitchin, Zecharia. 1980. *The Stairway to Heaven*. New York: Avon.

Sitchin, Zecharia. 1985. *The Wars of God and Men*. New York: Avon

Sitchin, Zecharia. 1990. *The Lost Realms*. New York: Avon.

Sitchin, Zecharia. 1990. *Genesis Revisited*. New York: Avon.

Sitchin, Zecharia. 1993. *When Time Began*. New York: Avon.

Sitchin, Zecharia. 1995. *Divine Encounters*. New York: Avon.

Smith, George. 1880. *The Chaldean Accounts of Genesis — from the Cuneiform Inscriptions*. London: Sampson Low, Marston, Searle & Rivington.

Treumann, Rudolf 1993. "The Cognitive Map and the Dynamic of Information" in *The Evolution of Cognitive Maps — New Paradigms for the Twenty-First Century* (edited by Ervin Laszlo and Ignazio Masulli). Yverdon, Switzerland: Gordon and Breach Science.

Wolf, Fred Alan. 1988. *Parallel Universes: The Search for Other Worlds*. New York: Touchstone.

Zangger, Eberhard. 1992. *The Flood from Heaven*. Great Britain: Sidgwick & Jackson.

72

Madeleine Briskin attended Brown University where she obtained her doctorate in 1973. She was appointed to the faculty at the University of Cincinnati in 1973 where she is now carrying out her duties as a Professor of Geology. She pioneered a number of research projects in the new subdiscipline of Paleooceanography-Paleo-climatology. Her publications, which appeared in international and national scientific journals, contributed to a new understanding of air-sea interactions, the evolution of ocean and atmospheric circulation in geologic time, climatic changes, Ice Ages and their related causal mechanisms; her research led to the identification of the 430,000 ± years astronomical cycle and the unifying model for a Pulsating Earth. She has been invited for numerous interviews by newspapers, radio and television for her integrated views of global problems.

Abstract

The mysterious ancient 432,000 ± years cycle so elegantly reported by Zecharia Sitchin, in his 1993 book "When Time Began," and which until recently was perceived as an elusive construct of eastern religions, has been identified in several independent scientific studies in the geologic record and the celestial mechanics.

This cycle is the well recognized Astronomical quasi-periodic cycle of 430,000 ± years identified by Briskin (1975, 1981, 1990) in a number of independent paleooceanographic parameters derived from the Pacific and Atlantic sediments. Calculations in the celestial mechanics yielded an equivalent cycle of 413,000 ± years. The 432,000 ± years, the 430,000 ± years and the 413,000 ± years are one and the same Astronomical cycle born out of the Earth's Orbital parameters and ultimately integrated within the familiar Milankovitch band. Integrated scientific results have led to the proposition that the earth pulsates with a quasi-periodic cycle of 430,000 ±. Furthermore, this periodicity becomes the framework of a unifying model which lifts our understanding of the evolution of earth systems. In other words, this astronomically induced pulsation is ultimately responsible for dynamical changes in the solid earth, its fluid envelope (ocean/atmosphere), its fluid core and the matrix of life.

The physical signature of the 430,000 ± astronomical cycle is no longer in doubt. It is well defined within the bounds of our objective reality. The fascinating and intriguing questions to be considered are: How is this cycle generated? Can we translate its geologic signature into critical evidence attesting the existence of a 10th planet in our solar system? And if yes, the implications are impressive; indeed it would accentuate the nagging possibility of a significant connection between the proposed model of a pulsating earth and the 10th planet — Nibiru.

As suggested by Sitchin in the Earth Chronicles, Nibiru is responsible not only for the creation of Earth but for the planetary orbits and a number of anomalies in our planetary system. According to Sitchin's theory Nibiru continues to exert a profound influence upon the solar system; in particular, Sitchin makes the bold assertion that the precession of the equinoxes can best be explained by the influence of Nibiru.

Chaotic events and pulsations in the solar system are not rare. But a major question arises, what is the singular role of Nibiru?

THE 430,000 ± YEARS PULSATION OF EARTH:

IS THERE A 10th PLANET CONNECTION?

by

Madeleine Briskin, Ph.D.

Cyclic changes in the Earth's orbital parameters which consist of the precession of the equinoxes (26,000 ± years), the obliquity (40,000 ± years) and the eccentricity of the orbit (100,000 ± years) are thought to be responsible for dynamical forcing of earth systems. Of particular interest is the well recognized 430,000 ± years quasi-astronomical cycle hidden in the variable amplitudes of the earth's eccentric orbit (Briskin et al 1975; Briskin et al 1980). Integrated geologic results presented in this paper should demonstrate the considerable significance of the 430,000 ± years cycle and underscore the "cosmic" connection between astronomical events and earth bound systems; of particular interest are this cycle's connection to dynamical events in the solid earth, its fluid core, its fluid surface envelope (atmosphere and ocean) and the inescapable connection to the diversity of life (Briskin et al 1989, 1990). The signal is identified in a number of independent paleooceanographic and geophysical parameters derived from the Atlantic and Pacific ocean sediments.

Analysis of data ultimately led to the development of a unifying planetary model for a *Pulsating Earth*. A possible connection to a 10th planet is explored; a 10th planet is herein called Nibiru in recognition of Zecharia Sitchin's provocative and scholarly works "The Earth Chronicles."

Copyright © Madeleine Briskin, 1996

The 430,000 ± quasi-astronomical cycle

First a brief exposé as to why oceanic sediments are so especially useful in recording the physical reality of astronomical cycles.

The earth's oceans which claim 70% of the earth's surface are coupled to the atmosphere; thus any secular perturbations in the atmosphere such as global temperature or climatic changes will consequently trigger a response in the oceanic circulation regime. While the atmosphere has a short memory, on the order of a few days, the ocean's memory encompasses 800 to 1,200 years. The underlying network of this memory is the microscopic single shell planktonic organisms which thrive in the upper water in distinct associations with currents and water mass boundaries. They live and die in the surface-water, recording environmental conditions at the surface. Upon their death their shells, which consist of the mineral calcite ($CaCO_3$) produce the perennial "carbonate snow" which settles on the ocean floor, forming vast accumulation of soft unconsolidated sediments called oozes; and because they live in the upper waters their ecology may be decoded in ways which provide the fundamental data to our overall understanding of causal models. The evidence introduced below was obtained from Atlantic and Pacific deep-sea sediments covering the last two million years (Pleistocene and Holocene) and also from an outcrop of shallow-water strata bordering the Gulf of Mexico covering 4.6 million years of Paleocene time.

Evidence: Atlantic and Pacific Oceans

1. Planktonic Assemblages

Deep sea fossil plankton were retrieved from the ocean floor at 15° North latitude in the Atlantic and 3° North latitude in the Pacific. These latitudes represent the tropical subtropical climatic zones. A quantitative analysis yielded a record of winter and summer temperature variations of the last two million years (Briskin et al 1975; Briskin et al 1980). The winter temperature designated as T_W clearly shows a pattern of large oscillations with periodicity of $430,000 \pm$ years (Fig. 1 & 2). This curve represents the first quantitative evidence for a $430,000 \pm$ year periodicity and its clear association with the history of ice ages in the Pleistocene. An obvious correlation exists between the eccentricity maxima of the middle curve derived from the celestial mechanics curve on the right and the oscillations along the winter temperature in the tropical Atlantic. The signal was similarly obtained in the fossil planktons of the Pacific.

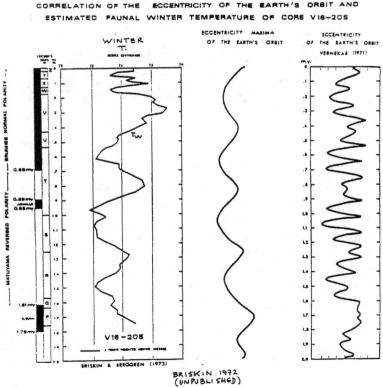

CORRELATION OF THE ECCENTRICITY OF THE EARTH'S ORBIT AND
ESTIMATED FAUNAL WINTER TEMPERATURE OF CORE V16-205

Figure 1

76

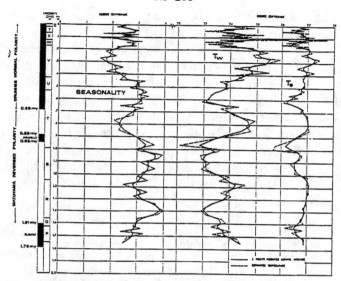

Graph showing the faunal indices Tw and Ts of estimated temperatures and the seasonality (Ts-Tw) plotted versus time. The dashed line represents the estimated temperature in degrees Centigrade, and the solid line is a three points weighted moving average of the estimated temperatures. Paleomagnetic boundaries and Ericson's faunal zones are inserted near the time scale in m.y. Four major roughly symmetrical climatic cycles are detected in Tw. Lowest estimated winter temperatures occur near the base of the Jaramillo, the warmest estimated winter temperatures in the mid and upper Brunhes. The three points weighted moving average (solid curve) delineates the major temperature pattern. The seasonality shows an inverse trend to Tw and Ts. (Briskin etal 1975)

Figure 2

2. Geochemical

Oxygen isotopic ratios obtained from the shells of fossil plankton offer additional independent evidence. Oxygen 16 is more abundant in nature than oxygen 18. During ice ages the oxygen 16 which is lighter than oxygen 18 is preferentially transported by water vapor to the high latitudes where it precipitates as snow, which eventually converts to continental ice.

Consequently, the oceans become enriched in oxygen 18. The plankton need an oxygen to precipitate their calcitic ($CaCO_3$) shells and of necessity will more commonly select oxygen 18. The ratio of $^{18}O/^{16}O$ obtained from fossil plankton shells are a proxy indicator of the amount of ice trapped on the continents; in other words the ratio is a good "thermometer" of climatic changes.

During the last Ice Age, which peaked at 18,000 years before present, 135 meters of sea water was evaporated and trapped in continental glaciers. Again a quantitative analysis of the $^{18}O/^{16}O$ ratios in both oceans yielded the 430,000 ± years cycle.

3. The Magnetic Field

To create a magnetic field you need a spinning planet with a liquid core. The earth's field is considered to be a self-sustaining dynamo and is understood to have been a dipole for at least 1 billion years and perhaps longer.

The magnetic field is characterized by three parameters: 1) the intensity or field strength measured in milligauss, 2) the declination which is the angle between the magnetic pole and the spin-axis (geographic pole), and 3) the inclination which describes the spatial geometry of the force field.

Over the equatorial regions the lines of force flow parallel to the earth. But with increasing latitude they begin to bend relative to the earth's surface until, at the magnetic North Pole, they are normal to the earth's surface (90° angle); at the magnetic North Pole they plunge into the earth towards the South Pole where they emerge diverging into space creating a "magnetic umbrella" which girdles the earth and shields it from the relentless solar wind and cosmic rays.

Of the three parameters tested only the inclination (Briskin 1979 unpublished) yielded the 430,000 ± years cycle. In the Pacific no signal emerged. And, indeed had it been otherwise the magnetic data would have been unacceptable; because at 3° North latitude, so close to the equator, the inclination is zero.

Those exciting serendipitous results were the first steps ultimately leading to the realization and conception of a pulsating earth model.

4. Sea Level Movements (Transgressions — Regressions)

The shallow-water sedimentary deposits of Paleocene rocks

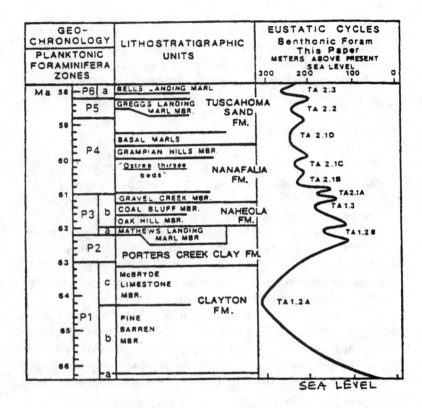

FIGURE 3—The paleoecologic-paleoceanographic signal based on benthic foraminifera assemblages is plotted in the context of the biostratigraphy which is calibrated to the geochronology of Berggren et al., 1985.

FIGURE 3

bordering the Gulf of Mexico preserve a record of strand line (shore line) displacement covering 4.6 million years of sea level history. Nine sea level movements (transgression — regression) with oscillations lasting 430,000 ± years were identified in this record (Fig. 3). The amplitudes between pulses mark the height of sea level encroachment over time.

Unlike the Pleistocene epoch which recorded drops in sea level (eustatic changes) caused by the buildup of continental ice, the

Paleocene epoch was basically an ice free world, with insignificant amounts of polar ice. What then caused sea level to oscillate with such regularity? Certainly not ice! The only logical conclusion must be the earth itself.

Periodicity

How real is the 430,000 ± cycle? Could it have occurred by chance alone?

The numerous independent parameters discussed above, each and every one yielding the 430,000 ± years cycle, is strong evidence against a chance occurrence. The results of several power spectral analyses (Briskin et al 1980, More et al 1982) showed power concentrated at the 430,000 ± years range. Calculations in the celestial mechanics (Berger 1977) yielded an equivalent cycle of 413,000 ± years. Stothers (1986, 1987) at the Goddard Institute for Space Studies tested the reality of a number of cycles derived from the fossil records and celestial mechanics; several were rejected as noise with the exception of the 430,000 ± years cycle.

Subsequent studies probing deeper in geologic time found the signal in Cretaceous rocks (Herbert and Fisher 1986) — a time when the earth was devoid of ice; the cycle was also observed in lake sediments of Triassic age (Olsen 1986), in Searles Lake (Philips pers. comm.) and other continental deposits (Renault pers. comm.). It is clearly evident that the cycle appears in marine and continental sediments of many ages.

The physical signature of the 430,000 ± cycle is well defined within the boundary of our objective reality. The 430,000 ± years and 413,000 ± years periodic cycle are one and the same cycle in the Milankovitch band; although as a point of scholarship and as a matter of record it must be stated that Milankovitch did not identify it.

A Pulsating Earth: A Unifying Planetary Model

What does this ubiquitous cycle's presence in different earth systems signify? How does one reconcile a signal associated with Pleistocene Ice Ages and sea level movements in the ice free world of the Paleocene? What common association, if any, is there with the magnetic field? The obvious overwhelming conclusion is that at the first order level, the earth systems were responding to one and only one forcing mechanism — the astronomical mechanism.

The proposed explanation is that both the fluid envelopes, the ocean and atmosphere, and the fluid core respond independently to the astronomical forcing.

The earth's orbit does not only stretch from near circularity to maximum eccentricity in $100,000 \pm$ years but the plane of its orbit precesses through space. It is this combination of relative motion around the sun's barycenter which generates the 430,000 $\pm$ years cycle. The cycle is a "beat" in the eccentricity of the orbit. It forces a response in the atmosphere/ocean system expressed in the realignment of isotherms and the circulation system. The shift may be of such a nature as to trigger the onset of ice ages.

Pulsations in the liquid core generate phase changes at the liquid core-mantle interface stimulating volumetric changes in the liquid (expansion/contraction). Thermal convection within the mantle may be intensified or weakened translating into vertical movements at the earth's surface which in turn cause the displacement of crustal plates; advective motions of the crustal plates are a secondary effect.

The geometry and rotational motion of plate interactions may well overprint the first order effect — the vertical movements.

Current plate tectonics models have been unable to adequately explain the occurrence of crustal flexure on the continents.

Sea level movements are not constrained by geometry and respond directly to the pulsations of the liquid core. It is why sea level movements with periodic oscillations of 430,000 ± years are clearly recorded in an ice free world.

If the heart of the planet is its core, its pulse is defined by the magnetic inclination, which expresses a 430,000 ± years periodicity.

It is reasonable to assume that the center of mass for the earth-moon systems must be displaced with the same periodicity; and that geophysical and geochemical events in the upper mantle (400 to 600 km) may be responding to this motion. Tidal frictions may be relaxed or intensified.

The Astronomical Connection

In the words of S. Gould "the fate of all species is extinction." And nowhere is it better expressed than the fossil record of the last 700 million years. In fact the definition of time horizons delineating particular geologic periods or eras relies uniquely on distinct discontinuities in the fossil assemblages which are understood to reflect major environmental changes at a given time horizon in the unfolding of earth history.

The consensus among earth scientists has always been that some of the extinctions were the natural outcome of biological and evolutionary processes forced by natural selection, the deciding factor in who lives and who dies. In the Darwinian model the fittest survives to reproduce descendants presumably "fitter" than themselves. Thus, the long stretch of geologic time was punctuated by communities of species which appeared, procreated and disappeared in a seemingly non-random cycle of creation and extinction.

The puzzle, however, is that some of these geologic boundaries define horizons of such extensive mortality that the term "mass extinction" was used to designate these global catastrophes. In particular the Permian-Triassic Boundary and the Cretaceous-Tertiary Terminal events stand out above the normal extinction pattern. Evidently variable frequencies of extinctions in fossil assemblages seem to record the signature of an external mechanism of global character which decimates the biosphere in catastrophic pulses of different intensities. The search for causal mechanisms divides efforts roughly into two camps — those researchers who seek earth-bound solutions (internal) and those who perceive that the answer may be found within events occurring in the solar system or at the Galactic level.

Until the Alvarez Model (1980) no mechanism, in particular, internal ones such as climate changes, sea level changes and tectonic upheaval, could adequately explain the pattern of "mass destruction" among marine and terrestrial life commonly referred to as the Cretaceous Terminal event. Alvarez's explanation was that 65 million years ago an asteroid ranging in size from 4 to 14 km in diameter collided with earth; it released an extraordinary amount of energy comparable to at least 100,000,000 megatons of TNT.

This extraordinary energy was absorbed by the earth and oceans and created super waves which crested at 5 km or more (Huggett 1989); the ocean surface boiled, a dark cloud of steam and pulverized earth debris was propelled into orbit; darkness enveloped the earth for a number of years. The shock wave and dissipative energy raised the temperature of the oceans and destroyed the structure of the atmosphere. Terrestrial vegetation burned out of control and the marine phytoplankton which supplied the bulk of the oxygen for the planet were nearly eliminated. The Alvarez Model was the "coup de grace" to the classical Darwinian view of evolution and shook the foundation of Lyellian uniformitarianism. It opened the door for a new understanding of the processes which shaped the earth and its biosphere. It became evident that cosmic phenomena were at work. A new paradigm was born. Comets shaped the solid earth and brought water which formed the oceans (Shoemaker, 1983). Comets carried the seeds of life from one world to another. Comets were the agents of creation and destruction. For the first time a correlation was established between extinctions, cratering events and the Solar System and Galaxy. Episodic patterns of cratering were detected on earth, the Moon, as well as other earth-like planets. It became obvious that a correlation existed between extinctions, cratering events, the Solar System and the Galaxy. The challenge was to seek out the cause of these episodic bombardments.

The Alvarez proposition captured the interest of scientists in numerous disciplines and sparked an ongoing vigorous debate which led to a number of creative theories, some in direct contradiction with one another. A number of statistical studies of the extinction and cratering records yielded several large periodicities — a 26 M year, 30 M year and a 40 M year cycle which held the promise of a solution. These were periodicities in "search" of a "cosmically correct" association — Nemesis, the Companion Star Solution (Raup & Sepkovski, Jr., 1986), the Solar Oscillations (Rampino and Stothers, 1984), the Comet Showers (Clube et al, p. 260) and Planet X (Anderson and Standish, 1986; Whitmore and Matese, 1985).

Unfortunately none of these proposed explanations survived the test of hypothesis. In some cases the problem rested with the lack of refinement in the extinction data, or error in statistical manipulations and unjustified assumptions about dynamical constraints in the Galactic and Celestial mechanical systems (Tremaine, 1986, p. 409), (Shoemaker and Wolfe, 1986, p. 338).

The tentative conclusion at this point is that no unique solution emerges which can explain the comet showers, bombardment, cratering frequencies, or extinction phenomena presumably tied to the 26 or the 30 million years cycle.

The Case for Planet X: Is Planet X Nibiru?

In the splendid and exhaustive work of Zecharia Sitchin's *Earth Chronicles* a planet called Nibiru, also called the Planet of the Crossing, is introduced as the eternal abode of the Gods. Its symbols are a disk with wings or a cross encoding the memory of its encounter with the primeval Solar System and primordial earth. In the Epic of Creation of Sumer, Nibiru and its suite of satellites wandered into the Solar System and across the chaotic orbit of the large undifferentiated planetesimal Tiamat (Earth). One of Nibiru's satellites collided with Tiamat, splitting it in half, creating the modern Earth and the Asteroidal belt between Mars and Jupiter. One of Tiamat's satellites became the moon. The event, according to Sitchin, stabilized the Earth's orbit in a way which set the pace for the precession of the equinoxes. The "Gods" defined the equinoctial cycle of 26,000 ± years (the Great Year) to create a pacemaker of time tuned to Nibiru's orbital time. The system was eventually impressed upon man and adopted by ancient Sumerian civilizations. The orbit of Nibiru is reported as 3,600 years.

If we're to accept Sitchin's thesis then Nibiru must have existed long before our Solar System. Where did it come from? Could it be a planet which survived the supernovae which created the cloud of cosmic dust which produced our Solar System? Or was it ejected from another solar system only to be captured by our solar system's gravitational force? Is there any supportive evidence that it is connected to our planetary destiny? Could it force a pulsation in the Earth? There are some interesting associations between the 430,000 ± years or 432,000 ± years (which are the same) and the planet Nibiru. The game is the following: If you divide 432,000 years by 3,600 years you obtain the number 120 which equals the number of sars reported by Sitchin. If you divide 432,000 years by 36,000 you obtain 12. This number is reminiscent of the 12 zodiacal signs in the precessional cycle; and in Judeo-Christian philosophy it is reminiscent of the 12 tribes and 12 apostles. 3,600 years multiplied by 10 results in 36,000, a cycle connected to the obliquity (tilt of the earth's axis) which is currently at 41,000 years; however, because the orbital parameters are quasi-periodic, the obliquity may vary from 36,000 years to 43,000 years.

This makes the 36,000 year cycle worthy of attention because a definite coupling is observed between the 432,000 years detected in the winter temperature (Fig. 2) and the obliquity of the Earth's orbit.

When multiplied by 1,000 the precessional cycle (26,000 years), and the obliquity cycle (36,000 or 43,000 years) equals 26,000,000 years, the 36,000,000 years and the 43,000,000 years cyclicity associated with the search for Planet X.

The existence of Planet X is still a point of debate and ardent research. Several studies have introduced evidence for its existence and claim it as the planet whose orbit perturbs the immense cometary disk extending in space beyond Pluto.

Harrington and Van Flandern (1978) postulate that certain anomalies in the Solar System could be best explained by a close encounter between the presence of a large planet of two to five earth masses. They further suggested that in the primordial days of the Solar System a single close encounter with an invading planet two to five times the mass of earth forced the simultaneous ejection of Pluto-Charon from the Neptunian satellite system, produced Triton's retrograde orbit and forced Nereid into its present, highly eccentric orbit. They calculated the planet's orbit to be at a distance of 50 to 100 AU and having eccentricity of less than 0.6. The idea was strengthened by Fernandez and Ip (1984) — who claimed that Planet Earth was perturbed to its present orbit in a close encounter with another planet of comparable mass.

Infrared Astronomical Satellite IRAS in a survey which covered most of the sky recorded a planet having three times the mass of the earth at a distance of 150 AU (Reynolds et al 1980).

Whitmore and Matese (1985 and 1986) postulated the existence of a tenth planet with mass one to five times the size of earth and whose orbits at a distance of 70 to 100 AU from the Sun was inclined 45° to the ecliptic. Its precessing Perihelion which advances every 26 to 30 million years passes twice through the Oört cometary cloud near the inner planets, causing the periodic displacement associated with the 26 to 30 million year cratering and extinction cycle. Planet X is assumed to be comparable to Neptune. Its albedo, although fainter than Neptune at greater distances, should be optically detectable and the failure to do so must be due to its large ecliptic inclination.

Cognard et al (1995) in their study of pulses emitted by rotating neutron stars, noted unexplained timing residuals in their data which led them to infer the presence of a massive 10th planet in orbit around the sun. However, they caution that small errors in the calculation of the mass and motion of known planets could mimic the gravitational effects of Planet X. Still they remain optimistic since their data are in close agreement with observations carried out at Arecibo, Puerto Rico. Additional information is expected over the next decade which may help resolve the uncertainties.

The numerical connections between the cycle of Nibiru and the geologic cycles reported in this paper are intriguing. It begs some explanation.

Since the first reported observations of planets in orbit around other star systems, astronomers have been identifying planets at the rate of one a month. And although the question of Planet X is unresolved the search has not abated and impending serendipitous results could resolve the mystery. Should this Planet be identified presently it ought to be justifiably called Nibiru S.Z. in honor of Zecharia Sitchin.

References

Anderson, J.D., and Standish, E.M., Jr., 1986, "Dynamical Evidence for Planet X," in *The Galaxy and the Solar System*, R. Smoluchowski, J.N. Bahcall, and M.S. Matthews, eds., U. of Arizona Press, p. 286.

Briskin, M., Fluegeman, R.E., Jr., and Berggren, W.A., 1989. "Paleocene Sea Level Movements: Evidence of Astronomical Forcing, Abstract, International Congress in Paleooceanography," University of Cambridge, England, September 10-16, 1989.

Briskin, M., and Berggren, W.A., 1975, "Pleistocene Stratigraphy and Quantitative Paleooceanography of Tropical North Atlantic Core," V. 16-205, In *Late Neogene Epoch Boundaries, Micropaleontology* Press, 167-198.

Briskin, M. and Harrell, J.," Time-Series Analysis of the Pleistocene Deep-Sea Paleoclimatic Record." *Journal of Marine Geology*, May 1980.

Briskin, M., and Fluegeman, R.E., Jr., "Paleocene Sea Level movements with a 430,000 Year Quasi-periodic Cyclicity," *Palaios*, Vol. 5, No. 2, Sept. 1990.

Clube, S.V.M. and Napier, W.M., 1986, "Grant Comets and the Galaxy: Implications of the Terrestrial Record," in The Galaxy and the Solar System, eds. R. Smoluchowski, J.N. Bahcall and M.S. Matthews, The University of Arizona Press, Tucson, pp. 1-415.

Cognard, I., et al, 1995, "High Precision Timing Observations of the Millisecond Pulsar PSR 1937+ 21 at Nansay," Astronomy and Astrophysics, Vol. 296, No. 1, pp. 171-178'

Davis, Hut, and Muller, 1984, "Extinction of Species by Periodic Comet Showers," *Nature*, Vol. 308, p. 715-17.

Harrington, R.A., and Van Flandern, T.C., 1979, "The Satellites of Neptune and the origin of Pluto." Icarus, Vol. 39, pp. 131-136.

Harrington, and van Flandern, 1978 in *The Galaxy and the Solar System*, R. Smoluchowski, J.N. Bahcall, and M.S. Matthews, eds., U. of Arizona Press.

88

Herbert, T.D., and Fisher, A.G., 1986, "Milankovitch Climatic Origin of Mid-Cretaceous Black Shale Rythms in Central Italy," *Nature,* V. 321, p. 732-743.

Huggett, R., "Cataclysms and Earth History," The Development of Diluvialism, Clarendon Press, Oxford, 1989, p. 1-215.

Kenneth, J.P., 1987, "Proceedings of the Ocean Drilling Program," Leg 113, Dec. 1986-March 1987, V. 113, p. 785 (pers. comm.).

Matese, J.J., and Whitmore, D.P., 1986, in *The Galaxy and the Solar System,* R. Smoluchowski, J.N. Bahcall, and M.S. Matthews, eds., U. of Arizona Press, p. 1-415.

Moore, T.C., Jr., Pisias, N.G., and Dunn, D.A., 1982, "Carbonate Time Series of the Quaternary and Late Miocene Sediments in the Pacific Ocean: A Spectral Comparison," *Marine Geology,* V. 46, p.217-222.

Olsen, P., 1986, "A 40 Million Year Lake Record of Early Mesozoic Orbital Climatic Forcing," *Science*, V. 234, p. 842-848.

Philips, F.M., (pers. comm.), New Mexico Institute of Mining and Technology, Sorocco, New Mexico, 87801.

Renault, J.R., (pers. Comm.), New Mexico Institute of Mining and Technology, Sorocco, New Mexico, 87801.

Rampino, M.R., and Stothers, R.B., 1984. "Terrestrial Mass Extinction, Cometary Impacts and the Sun's Motion Perpendicular to the Galactic Plane," *Nature*, Vol. 309, p. 709-712.

Raup, D.M., and Sepkovski, J.J., Jr., 1986, Periodic Extinctions of Families and Genera, Science, p. 833-836.

Raup, D.M., 1986a, *The Nemesis Affair*, W.W. Norton and Co., New York, London.

Reynold, R.T., Tarter, J.C., and Walker, R.G., 1980, "A Proposed Search of the Solar Neighborhood for Substellar Objects." Icarus, Vol. 44, p. 772-779.

Schlanger, S.O., 1986, "High Frequencies Sea Level Fluctuations in Cretaceous Time: An Emerging Geophysical Problem in Mesozoic and Cenozoic Oceans." Hsu, K.J., *Geodynamic Series*, V. 15, p. 61-74.

Sepkovski, J.J., Jr., and Raup, D.M., 1986, "Periodicity in Marine Extinction Events in Dynamics of Extinction," K. Elliott, Ed., John Wiley and Sons, New York, pp. 1-36.

Shoemaker, E.M., and Wolfe, R.F., 1986, Asteroid and Comet Bombardment of the Earth," Earth Planet Science, Annual Review, Vol. 11, pp. 461-494.

Shoemaker, E.M., and Wolfe, R.F., 1986, "Mass Extinctions, Crater Ages and Comet Showers," in *The Galaxy and the Solar System*, R. Smoluchowski, J.N. Bahcall, and M.S. Matthews, eds., U. of Arizona Press, p. 338.

Sitchin, Z., 1993, "When Time Began," United Press International, pp. 410.

Stothers, R.B., 1987, "Beat Relationships Between Orbital Periodicities in Insolation Theory," *Journal of Atmospheric Science*, V. 44, p. 1875-1876.

Stothers, R.B., 1986, "Periodicity of the Earth's Magnetic Reversals," *Nature*, V. 322, p. 444-446.

Tremaine, S., 1986, Is there Evidence for a Solar Companion?, in *The Galaxy and the Solar System*, R. Smoluchowski, J.N. Bahcall, and M.S. Matthews, eds., U. of Arizona Press, p. 409.

Whitmore, D.P., and Matese, J.J., 1985, "Periodic Comet Showers and Planet X," *Nature*, Vol. 313, p. 36-46.

V. Susan Ferguson was born on December 6, 1945, and grew up in Texas. She lived in New York City for twenty years studying painting and metaphysics. She attended Parson's School of Design and has a BFA in Painting. In 1995 she wrote *Inanna Returns* (Thel-Dar Publishing Co.), and the sequel, *Inanna Hyper-Luminal,* in 1996. V. Susan Ferguson lives in Seattle, WA, with her husband.

INANNA RETURNS
by
V. Susan Ferguson

A tablet from Uruk in the Louvre Museum describes Inanna, the delightful and highly imaginative great-granddaughter of Anu, as ". . . clothed with love, feathered with seduction, a goddess of joy," (Sitchin, 1995, page 167). Inanna is unquestionably one of the most engaging and colorful members of the family of Anu, and Zecharia Sitchin's recent books have played a major part in Inanna's return to the 20th century.

In 1990 I read Zecharia Sitchin's *The Wars of Gods and Men*. As I read the chapters on Inanna, I began to experience her life in full living color as if I were Inanna in a holographic moving picture. For example, I found myself standing beside the Great Pyramid at Giza wearing a golden warrior's outfit; I struck those enormous stones with a sword-like laser beam and cheerfully shouted obscenities at my cousin Marduk.

Inanna's life thus unfolded before me and I began to have visions of Nibiru, her home planet. I, as Inanna, felt myself to be a little girl running through the Halls of Anu's palace on Nibiru. I was laughing and running for the sheer joy of it; everyone loved me. The palace was an open pavilion with highly polished floors of lapis-lazuli and tall columns of malachite and marble, which were interspersed by white billowing curtains hung from the high ceilings. A gentle breeze caressed my black curls; I looked down at my chubby baby feet and saw that they were blue. In my experience, the color of Inanna's skin was a lovely creamy turquoise blue much like the color used in the paintings of India's Lord Krishna.

Copyright © V. Susan Ferguson, 1996

My impressions of Inanna and her family unfolded in what might be termed an *"altered state"* experience while I read Mr. Sitchin's books, also in the dream state, and during meditation. These visions continued off and on for a period of about six months. I have practiced meditation for many years and the visionary experience is not new to me; however, living Inanna's life was new, and quite an exhilarating adventure.

My modern state of mind was noticeably timid and narrow compared to Inanna's. I felt the awesome power of her self-confidence, based on an overwhelming abundance of love from her family which she took for granted. As Inanna, I possessed an intimate understanding of the other members in the family of Anu; I felt a relaxed familiarity which only exists with those one has grown up with.

Within the context of my visions, Inanna's relationship with Anu is somewhat difficult to describe because of the extreme differences in our modern day cultural values. Inanna (Ishtar) ". . . with Anu together occupying the closed-off Gigunu, the Chamber of Joy, as the other gods stand in front" (Sitchin, 1995, page 167). In the Gigunu, the Chamber of Joy, Anu enjoyed a sacred sexual experience with his great-granddaughter in which, from my understanding, they became one being. Sex was much more than a physical act for Inanna and Anu, and the other gods. The sexual experience was a merging of energies on many levels which enhanced the creative powers of both partners and the aggregate of their race. This knowledge has been lost, and perhaps purposively so, to us as twentieth century humans.

". . . as the other gods stand in front" (Sitchin, 1995, page 167). Not only did Antu, Anu's sister/wife, and the other gods not mind Inanna's coupling with Anu, rather they were delighted. They knew that the fusion of these two, as archetypal polarities, would provide them all with an expanded consciousness. The sexual experience was considered an art form which enhanced life on many levels. My understanding is that Inanna learned the Arts of Love from Antu. Inanna was the Antu's favorite pupil, not only because she was her adorable great-granddaughter; but also because Inanna was a natural, born to love and be loved.

"Enki and Inanna drank beer together . . .
They drank more and more beer together . . .
They toasted each other; they challenged each other."
(Wolkstein, 1983, page 14).

Inanna's relationship with Enki, her grandfather Enlil's half-brother, is well documented in Mr. Sitchin's books. Inanna used her considerable charms to trick Enki out of the Divine *ME's* so that she could build her territories into "full-fledged centers of urban civilization." (Sitchin, 1995, page 168).

Enki, as I have seen him, is a true connoisseur of women who thoroughly appreciated Inanna's wit and beauty; the two enjoyed each other's sense of humor and company. I felt that Inanna finally agreed to marry Enki's son, Dumuzi, because of her fondness for Enki. In spite of the many hymns which celebrate her supposedly romantic marriage to Dumuzi, Inanna considered him vain and dull; and contrary to recorded laments, was not exactly displeased by his death.

Inanna was the kind of girl who liked to move on in her life; stagnation had no appeal for her. The Right of bestowing Kingship gave Inanna an outlet for her many talents. "Enlil assigned to the goddess Ishtar (his granddaughter) the task of finding a suitable candidate for the first throne in the City of men — Kish, in Sumer." (Sitchin, 1995, page 110).

The fact that Enlil gave Inanna this crucial job shows that even Enlil respected Inanna's gifts. What magical powers did she possess? The ability to assess a man's strengths and weakness, his intelligence and integrity? Today the Arts of Love as were practiced by Inanna's priestesses in her temples are rarely known; they encompass far more than the physical act of sexual union.

Another very powerful memory I experienced through Inanna was the Great Flood, Enlil's bright idea to eliminate the human population. The memory begins with Inanna being informed of the coming deluge whose cataclysmic proportions she had yet to comprehend. Her friend and pilot Nungal had come to fetch her. ". . . Nungal, the Lion-hearted was the Pilot who from the skies brought Ishtar down to the E-Anna. (Sitchin, 1985, page 237).

Nungal urges her to hurry, but Inanna hasn't had time to pack and is transfixed by her massive quantities of jewels which she is reluctant to leave behind. In the typical adolescent narcissism so characteristic of the family of Anu, Inanna cannot make up her mind what to take; and like a child, throws golden crowns and necklaces of diamonds, rubies, and pearls from one trunk to another until Nungal finally convinces her that her life is in danger and drags her, along with a heavy trunk bulging with treasure, out of her rooms.

Once in the ship high above the Earth, Inanna begins to realize the immensity of what is happening. "Ishtar cried out like a woman in travail: 'The olden days are alas turned to clay.' . . . The Anunnaki gods weep with her. The gods, all humbled, sit and weep; their lips drawn tight . . . one and all." (Sitchin, 1976, page 398). Inanna looks below and sees the Earth being covered by massive tidal waves. Inanna is genuinely bewildered by the desperate prayers of the priestesses in her temples begging her to save them. As if remote viewing, she watches them drown; their white gowns float for a brief moment before they are covered by a watery grave.

"Forced to abandon Earth, they (the gods) suddenly realized how attached they had become to it and its inhabitants." (Sitchin, 1976, page 399). Inanna and Ninharsag hold on to each other and cry inconsolably. "Ninti (Ninharsag) wept and spent her emotion; . . . she was overcome with grief.' (Sitchin, 1976, page 398). Ninharsag realized how much she had grown to love the lulus; she felt as if the race that she and Enki had created were like her own children.

"The Goddess saw and she wept . . .
her lips were covered with feverishness . . .
'My creatures have become like flies —
they filled the rivers like dragonflies,
their fatherhood was taken from them by the rolling sea.'"
(Sitchin, 1976, page 398).

Inanna's memories of Sargon were particularly vivid, perhaps because Sargon came very close to fulfilling Inanna's romantic dreams. After Gilgamesh had rejected and publicly insulted Inanna, she was all the more determined to find her Mr. Right. Perhaps she saw Sargon through rose colored glasses; but what is romantic love after all if not a fleeting, delicious, and not-to-be-missed illusion?

Sargon reminded Inanna of her father and according to the memories she shared with me, Sargon had Nannar/Sin's beguiling eyes.

"Sargon, the mighty king of Agade, am I.
My mother was a high priestess; I knew not my father."
(Sitchin, 1985, page 246).

The men in the family of Anu had a roving eye and a taste for the ladies; and Inanna's father, Nannar/Sin, was no different in this respect as is well documented by the existence of Inanna's somewhat estranged half-sister, the dazzling Ereshkigal. Nannar could have fathered Sargon by a seductive high priestess.

Another fact points to the possibility of Sargon being an offspring of Nannar/Sin. Enlil, as Nannar/Sin's father, would quite naturally take an interest in his half-grandson; and it was Enlil who gave Sargon lordship and kingship. "Sargon's records of his conquest describe Inanna as actively present on the battlefields but attribute to Enlil the overall decision regarding the scope of the victories and the extent of the territories: 'Enlil did not let anybody oppose Sargon, the king of the land; from the Upper Sea to the Lower Sea Enlil gave unto him.'" (Sitchin, 1985, page 249).

Inanna's visual memories of Sargon center around an enormous cedar bed which the two lovers slept on. As I looked out an open window at the shimmering city of Agade, I saw the same image of white billowing curtains I had seen on Nibiru. The couple apparently shared an abundance of sexual happiness together that included some significant transformations in Sargon's consciousness, and perhaps in his DNA, because of this union with Inanna.

Time did not stand still for the half-son of Nannar/Sin and while Inanna remained in her prime, as gorgeous and enticing as ever, Sargon began to age. This was a problem Inanna continually had to face, much like the Highlander in today's television series. Sargon couldn't handle this ineluctable and tragic reality; he began to drink excessively. To make matters worse, Sargon made the dreadful mistake of insulting Enki's son, Marduk; Sargon "took away soil from the foundation of Babylon and built upon the soil another Babylon beside Agade." (Sitchin, 1985, page 250).

"On account of the sacrilege Sargon thus committed,
the great lord Marduk became enraged
and destroyed his people by hunger.
From the east to the west he alienated them from Sargon;
and upon him inflicted as punishment that he could not rest."
(Sitchin, 1985, page 250).

Inanna watched helplessly as the man she had once loved passionately crumbled into a pathetic drunk afflicted by insomnia and tormented by demons. In his wretchedness, Sargon cursed her before he died. The death of Sargon marked the end of Inanna's adolescence.

A more cheerful image of Inanna is the one of her riding her pet lion wearing some of her most inspirational clothing, or lack thereof, in front of her troops. After Sargon's death, Inanna was bitterly determined not to lose everything they had built together. The soldiers worshipped Inanna and she led them into battle with her beauty and courage.

Fearing that Inanna was beyond his control, her grandfather Enlil eventually turned against her and ordered his mountain troops, the Gutium hordes, to attack Akkad and wipe the glittering city built by Sargon and Inanna, Agade, off the face of the Earth. Inanna lost everything; in abysmal defeat the Queen of Heaven and Earth went home to her parents. The words of Inanna's mother echoed in my heart: "Enough, more than enough innovations, O great queen!" (Sitchin, 1985, page 261).

Five years after my *"altered-state"* experience of tapping into Inanna's memories, I wrote her story from her point of view. I published *Inanna Returns* in May of 1995 and began to travel around the country introducing her book. To my amazement, I discovered that I wasn't the only one Inanna and the family of Anu were in "communication" with. My first encounter was with a woman who told me she had never seen Inanna's name in print before; yet, in her meditation a beautiful lady had appeared to her and called herself Inanna.

In Santa Fe, a woman told me that while she was reading Mr. Sitchin's *Wars of Gods and Men,* she recalled being one of the "birth-goddesses," one of the nurses who had volunteered to incubate the lulu fetuses. She told me that this was the most vivid and painful memory of all her past lives because the babies were taken from them over and over again. The fate of the babies was not made known to these nurses/birth-goddesses and they rightly suspected some of them were being destroyed. They were told by Ninharsag and Enki, that "It was for the good of their planet Nibiru." This woman told me that whenever she recalled this memory, she still felt emotionally bitter.

I was also in Santa Fe when, after giving a lecture about Inanna, I looked up and saw that half the people in the room were crying. The men and women were overcome with emotion; they remembered assisting Inanna in her Temples of Love. I have found it very interesting that almost as many men seem to be interested in *Inanna Returns* as women; although, knowing Inanna, perhaps I should not be too surprised.

Many other people have reported their experiences with the family of Anu to me; some of which occurred while they were reading Mr. Sitchin's books, and some before the books were published. Many people identified with one specific member of the family of Anu, such as Ninharsag, Anu, Enki, or Inanna; others simply felt that they had actually been one of the Anunnaki present at the initial colonization of the planet Earth.

All of these people felt a strong connection with the experiences described in the cuneiform tablets as translated by Zecharia Sitchin; and all of them feel that they are somehow still connected and living out the closure of this experience.

Mr. Sitchin's latest book, *Divine Encounters,* was particularly intriguing for me. The book deals with the historical evidence of the frequent encounters in the ancient world of humans with the so-called "gods," a phenomenon I felt I was experiencing along with the many others who had shared their recent Divine Encounters with me.

Here was extensive documented evidence of the interaction between the gods and men which had taken place either in the dream state or as visions. These Divine Encounters had often changed the course of history; kings had been given their power to win wars and visions to build empires. Religions were created and sanctified by such experiences. Temporarily, the veils were lifted.

Why do we no longer see the "gods"? Why do our myths contain endless descriptions of genies, elves, fairies, and other beings which are now invisible to us? In the *Mahabharata*, the great Hindu epic, there are the gods and the antigods; within the category of antigods are genii, giants, the stellar spirits, the demons of Time, threshers, serpents, wearers of impenetrable armor, eaters of raw flesh, and night wanderers.

In the third book of the *Mahabharata*, the *Book of the Forest,* Matali, Indra's charioteer, and Arjuna describe an airborne city.

"This lovely airborne city, with the splendor of good works, piled with all precious stones and impregnable even to the Immortals, the bands of Yaksas and Gandharvas, and Snakes, Asuras, and Raksasas, filled with all desires and virtues, free from sorrow and disease was created . . . " (van Buitenen, 1975, page 549).

". . . because of a boon given them the Daityas (genii) easily held their celestial, divinely effulgent, airborne city, which could move about at will. Now it would go underground, then hover in the sky, go diagonally with speed, or submerge in the ocean." (van Buitenen, 1975, page 550).

Are all these beings and descriptions of flying cities merely the product of the human imagination, and what is imagination? *The Oxford Etymological Dictionary* (1974) defines the word imagine as "to conceive of, think, devise," from the Latin stem *"imago, a likeness."* A likeness from where or what? Where do the images we imagine come from? No one has ever defined the human imagination; and yet, we all admire someone with a vivid imagination. We say they are highly imaginative, or they have no imagination. Imagination is something we value; and yet, its source remains a mystery.

Carl Gustav Jung speaks of his conversations with a "being" he calls Philemon, a fantasy figure ". . . in the psyche . . . which produce themselves and have their own life . . . It was he who taught me psychic objectivity, the reality of the psyche . . . Philemon represented superior insight." (Jung, 1965, page 183). Jung also speaks of his visions: "Those inner states were so fantastically beautiful that by comparison this world appeared downright ridiculous . . . those visions . . . were the most tremendous things I have ever experienced." (Jung, 1965, page 295).

The theory of Cycles, or *Yugas,* is described in the *Mahabharata.* Four Yugas make up the duration of a day for Brahma, the creative principle. The first period is called the Krita Yuga in Sanskrit, or the Age of Wisdom; the second, the Treta Yuga or the Age of Ritual, is a time when ritual replaces wisdom. The third age is termed the Dvapara Yuga or the Age of Doubt.

The fourth and final age is the Kali Yuga, or the Age of Conflict. The *Mahabharata* and the *Puranas* contain lengthy descriptions of the events which take place during the Kali Yuga. Along with the usual predictions of disasters, floods, and famines is the diverting notion that "Ready-cooked food will be on sale." (*Linga Purana,* chapter 40; Danielou, 1987, page 212). Our modern fast food restaurants may be telling us something.

Zecharia Sitchin asserts that the Nefilim measured time in a different way than we do; 3,600 of our Earth years are only one year, termed a *shar,* for the family of Anu. The recent developments in Quantum physics have allowed a greater flexibility in our thinking and today people commonly consider time as relative.

Quantum realities such as: "There is no deep reality. There is no quantum world. There is only an abstract quantum description." (Herbert, 1985, page 16, 17), "Reality is created by observation." (Herbert, 1985, page 17), and "Consciousness creates reality." (Herbert, 1985, page 24), can also apply to the way we experience time. The perception of time is relative to individual consciousness.

Not only do the Nefilim experience time differently than we do, as Mr. Sitchin suggests; but perhaps we, who are now living in the twilight of the Kali Yuga, can only experience time through the filter of the mode which corresponds uniquely to that Yuga.

"Traditional man did not have the same experience of time as modern man; he had a supertemporal sense of time and in this sensation lived every form of his world." (Evola, 1995, page xxxii).

The Kali Yuga is considered to have begun around 3400 BC. Mr. Sitchin gives 3450 BC as the date for the Tower of Babel incident when the Anunnaki confused Mankind's languages.

"That there was initially a time when mankind 'spoke in unison' is a tenet of Sumerian historical recollections. These also assert that the confusion of languages, accompanying the dispersion of mankind, was a deliberate act of the gods." (Sitchin, 1985, page 198).

Could it be that the Kali Yuga began when "Marduk started a chain of events replete with tragedies." (Sitchin, 1985, page 199)? Perhaps Marduk played his part in initiating a fundamental change in our perceptions of time, and with this change, we human beings lost our ability to *see* the gods.

Trapped in the limiting time frequencies of the Kali Yuga, modern man is no longer able to perceive and communicate with other dimensional realities. *Divine Encounters* is the historical record of those who in their time were considered as the "great ones" who had retained, possibly through their genetic lineage, the ability to communicate with the gods or God, even if only in their dream state. No one dared to doubt that Abraham, Moses, or King David spoke to invisible beings.

"In traditional societies the 'invisible' was an element as real, if not *more* real, than the data provided by the physical senses." (Evola, 1995, page 4).

No one who has ever been to the Greek island of Delphi would underestimate the importance the ancient world placed on communication with the so-called '"invisible" world. The ancient Greeks, Chinese, Celts, and many others accessed knowledge from the "other side."

Lost in our miasma of electromagnetic waves, which constantly stream through us from our televisions, radios, and other sources, we as modern man and woman have not only come to deny the existence of the Invisible Worlds which support us; we have come to ridicule those who, for whatever reason, are receiving Divine Encounters.

The *Linga Purana* describes the world of Mahar, an extra planetary world, that some of the human species may take refuge in. When the "dissolution of the world seems imminent, some people abandon the earth during the last days of the Kalpa and take refuge in the world of Mahar (the extra planetary world) and from there will return to the 'world of life.'" (*Linga Purana;* Danielou, 1987, page 218). Could Mahar possibly be Nibiru?

Everyone asks Zecharia Sitchin when the planet Nibiru will orbit once again near the Earth. We may be better served by asking when will we, as the human species, be able to *see* Nibiru? When their Spanish conquerors first sailed into the coastal waters of Central America, the Indians living there were unable to "see" the ships because they did not recognize the existence of sailing ships.

Zecharia Sitchin has pursued his convictions undaunted by convention and dared to translate the cuneiform tablets as he saw them, a task well beyond most of our abilities. His courage and devotion to scholarship have opened the door to a greater understanding and the adventure that lies therein. Without Mr. Sitchin I never would have come to know the wonderful, beautiful, and irrepressible Inanna.

Perhaps Inanna and her family are already here whispering to us in our dreams and meditations, endeavoring to prepare us, along with Mr. Sitchin, for the future. As the Kali Yuga unwinds, perhaps the Veils, as frequencies of linear time which separate us from other dimensional realities, will lift and we will see unequivocally what has been around us all along.

References

Danielou, Alain, 1987. *While the Gods Play,* Shaiva Oracles and Predictions on the Cycles of History and the Destiny of Mankind. Inner Traditions International, Rochester, Vermont.

Evola, Julius, 1995. *Revolt Against the Modern World.* Inner Traditions, International, Rochester, Vermont.

Herbert, Nick, 1985. *Quantum Reality*, Beyond the New Physics. Anchor Press/Doubleday, Garden City, N.Y.

Jung, C.G., 1965. *Memories, Dreams, Reflections.* Vintage Books, New York.

Sitchin, Zecharia, 1976. *The 12th Planet.* Avon Books, New York, N.Y.

Sitchin, Zecharia, 1985. *The Wars of Gods and Men.* Avon Books, New York, N.Y.

Sitchin, Zecharia, 1995. *Divine Encounters.* Avon Books, New York, N.Y.

van Buitenen, J.A.B., 1975. *The Mahabharata,* Book 2, the Book of the Assembly Hall; and Book 3 The Book of the Forest. The University of Chicago Press, Chicago, IL. and London, England.

van Buitenen, J.A.B., 1978. *The Mahabharata*, Book 4, The Book of Virata; and Book 5 The Book of the Effort. The University of Chicago Press, Chicago, IL. and London, England.

Wolkstein, Diane, and Kramer, Samuel Noah, 1983. *Inanna. Queen of Heaven and Earth*, Her Stories and Hymns from Sumer. Harper & Row Publishers, New York, N. Y.

104

Neil Freer is a philosopher, writer, lecturer, and poet living in Santa Fe, NM. He holds a BA in English and did his graduate work in Philosophy and Psychology at the New School for Social Research. He has taught college courses in Philosophy and History of Religion, gives private and public seminars and lectures and has done over one hundred radio interviews. He is the author of *Breaking the Godspell* (New Falcon Publications, 3rd printing, 1994), a book which explores the ramifications of the archaeological, astronomical and genetic proof for our being a genetically engineered species and presents the ramifications of this new paradigm of human nature that resolves the Creationist-Evolutionist conflict. He is currently working on a second book, *God-Games,* in which he explores the ways in which we will live when, individually and collectively, we attain the unassailable integrity afforded by the restoration of our true genetic history. He outlines the racial maturity of the new planetary civilization and describes the new human.

FROM GODSPELL
TO GOD GAMES
by
Neil Freer

The planet is on hold because of the recycling of outmoded paradigms in all areas. In many respects we are faced with a near crisis of survival as a planetary race. But this is the end-game of an age, be certain. The lumbering lunatic caricature of the hapless hero with a thousand hangups is over: mark it well. Yet everyone knows that there is something grand about to happen! There is a new human emerging, a new planetary civilization on the horizon. We probe the elastic membrane of our racial imprints for the adequate maps and metaphors, the comprehensive unifying vision of the way beyond war, want, primitive competition, and the inevitability of death. But we reject partial solutions grasped at in the criteria vacuum conflict between religion, philosophy, science and new age hope. Yet there is an almost unthinkable new world-view dawning that releases us into that new era beyond religion and beyond the old new age. The background for the new paradigm comes from archaeology, bio-genetics, anthropology and astronomy.

We are profoundly indebted to the Sumerian scholar, Zecharia Sitchin, for his archaeological synthesis which proves the transcultural gods (Sumerian:Anunnaki; Egyptian:Neter; Hebrew:Anakim, Nefilim, Elohim), whom the ancient civilizations insisted came here from space, created humans and gave us civilization, were flesh and blood humanoids from the last planet in our solar system (Nibiru, Planet X) who genetically engineered us as slave animals by splicing their genes with Homo Erectus

Copyright © Neil Freer, 1996

genes and, eventually, accepted us as limited partners. That is the true "natural history of the gods" that Joseph Campbell failed. A half million pieces of archaeological proof are corroborated by the evidence for Planet X/Nibiru as developed by NASA, JPL, the Naval Observatory and various astronomers. Its gravitational pull on Uranus and Neptune flags it as being in our solar system. The mitochondrial DNA "search for Eve" and anthropology's "out of Africa" data placing our genesis in Central Africa 250,000 years ago, as well as strong evidence from many field of study, corroborate the ancient records.

Why should we accept this almost unthinkable history? The traditional belief has been that the "gods" must have been imaginary because the deeds (flight through the atmosphere and space, use of weapons akin to atomic bombs and star-war lasers, the ability to communicate over long distances, the ability to create humans) ascribed to them were utterly fantastic. That reasoning has been vaporized by our own current technological capabilities. Reaching the point in our technological knowledge that allows us to understand genetic engineering, lasers, interplanetary rocketry, electronic communication, has furnished the keys to the integration of our past with our present, encompassed in the concept of generic humanity — the critical factor for planetary unification. In this perspective, in every area, it becomes clear that almost every previous philosophical, religious, metaphysical and scientific world view has been partially correct.

The two major paradigms, the Creationist world view and the Evolutionary model, which have molded Western culture have been subsumed, corrected and outmoded by this new meta-paradigm of human nature provided by the profound ramifications of the new archaeological perspective. Joseph Campbell's gods are unmasked.

The Politics Of Our Evolution

The politics of our unique racial history may be characterized as a rapid evolution from slave to serf, to saviors to self. We were literally invented for the Nefilim pragmatic purposes as gold-mining and agricultural slave animals, became their serfs and limited partners with kings as local go-between foremen after they almost wiped us out in the Flood. Once they had phased off the planet and left us on our own, we began to look to charismatic saviors, political and eventually "religious," to lead us in the same submissive way we had formerly looked to our Nefilim masters. I feel fortunate to be living in and contributing to an age when we are emerging from racial adolescence.

We come alive in a laboratory, the mutant fusion of an alien race with slightly more advanced knowledge and science than ours is today, with an indigenous species with intelligence requiring genetic manipulation to bring it up to adequate for basic gold mining operations. We are slaves of these far superior masters, looking up, innocent, naked and history-less, in awe at their power, knowledge, history and amazing activities. As we develop over time, more precociously than they perhaps anticipated, some of us, at least, are recognized for a growing potential, elevated in status and function, sometimes even taken as sexual partners. Occasionally the offspring of such a marriage, like the king, Gilgamesh, who knew his mother to be pure Nefilim and his father human, demanded the rights of the Nefilim. Gilgamesh literally demanded immortality on a purely legal basis as a demi-god, a half-god. Surplus of us are pushed into the outback and develop our own adaptive native cultures from scratch. The out-backers retain some of the old memories from the masters' centers and hand them down as venerable, important, sacred.

And our own "religions," naive proto-scientific explanations of the awesome forces and mysteries of nature evolve over time, mix with the venerable traditions and legends. This "outlaw" culture spreads over the globe carrying with it the ancient history of our beginnings and the watershed events (the Orinoco Indians knew the Flood story. The American Indian cultures had 42 versions of it) and the veneration of the Nefilim Goddess Mother, Ninhursag, the Nefilim geneticist who literally made us. Gradually over time the two traditions con-fuse. But the "in-law" culture, still in direct contact with the Nefilim, know the masters to be flesh and blood humanoids and definitely in control. Kings are put in charge when the populations get large and the candidates for this foreman position are often very capable but aware of the danger of mistakes.

The rules are simple: do exactly as you are told as a foreman or you die, maybe be lucky and just get exiled. The Sumerian word for worship meant "work for," serve. And, from the beginning that we did, including acting our servant parts in the palace serving the masters the coq au vin, the beer, the wines they loved, the fatted calf, the bull and grains. When our females became attractive to the Nefilim males and they began to collect harems of these desirable female slaves and beget children by them we became too much of a nuisance-threat and the Nefilim attempted to wipe out all of us in the Flood and then rethought their decision. Having decided to keep us as valuable in rebuilding their centers after the devastating Flood, they taught us "crash courses" in civilization and technology as necessary for specific functions – farming, husbandry, textile production, food preparation, beer and wine production, mining, construction, slave raiding, scribing, keeping the calendar, knowing how to tell when the home planet, Nibiru, would again pass within the inner solar system and the Nefilim return.

Breaking The Godspell

And then they phased off the colony planet. Pretty much just left without closing the laboratory door, apparently beginning around 1250 B.C.. The foreman-kings are suddenly depicted in the stone carvings standing where they used to stand when listening to instructions from the master pointing to the master's now empty chair in utter dismay. The laments are still engraved in the clay tablets: "What do I do when my master is no longer here to instruct me . . . what shall I tell the people." We went into grief, despair, denial. We blamed ourselves and looked to the sky for their return. The good kings did their best, the leaders sometimes were told to go up the mountain to get some instructions long distance from space, or make a wooden box lined with metal just so, to act as a receiver. "Now hear this." Finally we were alone and in confusion, beginning to fight over who still knew what the master really said, really meant, what we really should be doing if he did show up. Service at their table transmuted into ritual sacrifice of food, attendance at their baths turned into bathing and clothing of surrogate statues of them and gradually the routine services turned into cargo-cult rituals and their palaces became empty temples. And the less than good kings began to take advantage, began to swagger. Sometimes they got away with it on their own. Sometimes the people, in desperation, raised their king to a symbolic god. And the god-king and the seed of the notion of the divine right of kings began. And the chief servants went along with it because it was to their advantage to become known as priests or to preserve their jobs and status. And those who had been taught, seeing that the advanced knowledge of technologies and science and the arts, learned as part of their function, of writing, mathematics, astronomy, science, metallurgy, and the fine crafts in general was being lost, set an agenda to preserve it. In the face of misunderstanding and threat they disguised it, withdrew it, hid it. And the "occult" became.

Eventually, the situation evolved to a very macabre stage. In an effort to demonstrate our subservience and zeal to make things right if they would just come back, we kept the rules, we maintained the routines of service but after a long time of disappointment we reached a point of abject, abysmal desperation where we would do anything to get them to come back – and we did. Remembering the Nefilim males' attraction to our young women, we began to cut their hearts out on top of the empty pyramidal palaces in a collective craven pleading shriek to the heavens from whence they had come and gone. But that unspeakable and unappreciated horror could not last: we began to doubt, to entertain frightening cynicism, secret thoughts of independence and "why bother."

Slowly a classic disassociational process developed due to separation in time and we began to sublimate the flesh and blood Nefilim into cosmic absolutes and their personalities into mythic archetypes. Looking back over the history of our species the traumatic transition we have gone through might well be characterized as the creation of the concept of a cosmic God by us, through a series of psychological mutational phases. Eventually, we simply began to forget.

The transition from racial amnesia to racial maturity has been a very traumatic passage. Breaking the godspell has seen us go through the stages of abandonment to disassociation, to sublimation to religion to rebellion and now to recovery. It is the classic syndrome of the dysfunctional family on a planetary scale.

Are we not haughty Egyptians, to whom the sky gods were everything, our rulers weakening and abandoned, now fearing that we had done something very wrong, searching the stars for some sign of their awesome craft? Are we not Hebrews, the chosen of our Nefilim master, Yahweh, preservers and transmitters of the advanced technological knowledge entrusted to us, becoming dismayed that the static is getting so bad that the words of the retreating Yahweh from the Ark loudspeaker can hardly be distinguished and Moses, the last to see him face to face is aging and even the nabi, the seers, argue about what he said? Are we not Innana's women of Mohenjo-Daro, for long sure of our dignity and her patronage, suddenly abandoned by our goddess queen? Are we not enlightened and democratic Greek citizens, logical people who could hardly accept the impossible deeds of the now-remote gods as anything but uncertain fantasies? Are we not Romans, sophisticated and urbane, masters of our destiny and the known world, would we give anything but lip service to the ancient deities now almost abstractions on our walls? Are we not Medieval Christian theologians already abstracting and sublimating the ruthless, peevish, jealous humanoid Nefilim Yahweh into an infinite, omnipotent, omniscient, cosmic being beyond our capabilities of thought who holds the universe in being just by thinking about it? Where was toil and danger? Down there slaving in the hot gold mines. And hell became. Where is the god and the good things that come from the god? Up there in the sky. And heaven became. Are we not the young Catholic priest telling his docile parishioners not to read the Old Testament and leave the interpretation of Scripture to the clergy trying privately in anguish to reconcile history with his faith? Are we not the fundamentalist bible school teacher watching herself mold the minds of children to a tradition of unquestioned docility to a God, her own doubts about whom she dare not allow herself to think?

And so, down to our day, incredibly, we have remained still Babel-factored for good crowd control, broken into tribes each proprietarily telling the other that ours is the only accurate tradition of what the god intended, what rules to follow, what we should be doing to demonstrate we are still loyal and docile servants. Sometimes we just kill each other over it. And persecutions, Crusades, Jihads, Inquisitions, evil empires, the saved and the damned, the martyr, the infidel, the saint, the Protestant, the fundamentalist, the atheist, became.

A very serious question is: Do other planets in other galaxies have the same overarching phenomenon of alien humanoid master/creators-> gods-> god-over-gods-> God-> GOD-> CREATOR OF UNIVERSES transformational sequence in their history because they were genetically engineered also? The convolution, sublimation, reverse anthropornorphizing (anyone have a better term for that? maybe anthropodeification?) intellectualizing, abstraction, that the notion of deity has gone through over the last 3000 years is, to be wryly positive about it, a tribute to human genius . . . .

On The Brink Of The New Paradigm

Where do we stand now in the transition?

One of the most intriguing indicators of where we are in the process of this coming out of the coma of racial amnesia to racial maturity is the current state of archaeology. Archaeology is on hold and in a state of quiet but desperate crisis. Robert Dunnell, a respected veteran archaeologist, said in an article in the January issue of Archaeology magazine entitled *Hope for An Endangered Science,* in 1989, ". . . intellectually, archaeology is in deep trouble, trouble that has been brewing for more than a century and has now reached crisis proportions." Most archaeologists would rather just dig and report and ignore the problems. Even those who are inclined to deal with the critical issues raised by the rapidly accumulating evidence for a new interpretation of the history of our species unfortunately tend to preclude even the possibility of the Nefilim presence. They instinctively realize that any retreat from the fundamental postulate that gods were myth, imaginary, unreal figments of naive human minds means revolution. For any serious scholar to even broach the possibility of "alien intervention" the price is most often peer persecution and even the ruin of one's career.

A reciprocal process has always been involved in our torturous coming to racial genetic enlightenment: the more we learn the freer and more confident we feel to learn and accept more, to shed the totems and taboos of the ancient godspell. At this point in time we quite clearly are reaching the point of radical paradigm shift. When we get this close to a paradigm shift changeover point everybody can feel it coming in their bones, in their genes, can almost taste it even though they may not be able to articulate it. So the predictions and the guesses and the prognostications about what the new paradigm really is are rife and various.

Some say, variously, the major changes will be focused around the shift into the precessional age of Aquarius: the paradigm shift is already on us and it means that the "vibrational level" of the entire planet will increase to a higher frequency generating a higher human consciousness; the actual crystalline form of the earth is shifting to a more complex form; the magnetic field of the earth is diminishing and magnetic pole reversals will trigger it; it will happen finally when aliens land and go public and, hopefully, offer us the solutions to all our problems; it's coming will be a monumental intellectual one as we decode the prophecies of the ancients; we will shift from the modern interpretation of the ancient world to a recognition of the identity, nature and advancement of the ancient civilization that gave rise to Sumer, Egypt, India, the Mayan empire and other western ancient empires.

Terence McKenna, having programmed the cycles of the I Ching into the computer (*Time Wave Zero*) can see a startling slide into novelty coming rapidly as we approach the year 2012 and sometimes says the paradigm shift will be a transcendental dimensional shift, that the world as we know it will end and sometimes says that he is not really sure. He, in one sense, is using the I Ching as a doomsday machine.

Some, like Marilyn Ferguson *(The Aquarian Conspiracy),* say that the big change is manifesting in a rising groundswell to a new level of human benevolence, kindness and love leading to a planetary order of peace. Some say that the paradigm shift will be more political, the manifestation of a New World Order leading to harmony and peace.

It takes little reflection to notice that the primary characteristic that dominates all these interpretations of these prophetic perceptions may be called, generically, a profound racial conscious-ness expansion. I suggest that what we are witnessing and experi-encing, in the largest perspective, is nothing less than the dawning of a planetary, racial, genetic enlightenment, that these gods, we and our children, wear designer genes, that we can and should claim our planetary birthright, restore our true collective history in the final dispelling of the haze of racial amnesia. We can inte-grate our indigenous heritage and become one with the earth again at the same time as we integrate our off-planet heritage and move off into space.

As we step out of racial adolescence, struggling through the awkward but inevitable separation from the parent-gods, now aware that our mythology is our greatest myth, we will realize that the myriad predictions, prophecies and pop-eyed pronounce-ments of turmoil, danger and glory are substantially correct pro-jections of the difficulties involved. The glimpses of glory are intuitive projections of the facets of the character and personality of the new planetary human and the new civilization already brim-ming over the horizon. The key to graceful passage is an unassail-able integrity, both racial and personal, springing from the genetic enlightenment that erases the painful scar of the subservient, godspell slave brand from our personal genetic web. We need, respectfully but firmly, to finally wash the ancient dyes of subjec-tion now sublimated to a focus on a pitifully anthropomorphic projection in the sky from the tapestries of our cultures.

Is this atheism? No. It simply is a long overdue correction of some local solar system politics, relatively rather pedestrian in cosmic perspective. Garden variety atheism can now be under-stood as an early sign of racial adolescent rebellion and question-ing of the authority of the obviously all too humanoid characteris-tics of the particular local Nefilim "god" of the Hebrew tribe and Christianity, Yahweh, who was, by his own admission, jealous (I am the Lord, your god, and you shall not go over the border and work for my brothers and cousins . . .) and clearly male chauvinist and disposed to violence in dealing with his human slaves if the high-tech tricks of magic and high wattage loudspeakers to which he resorted to intimidate them didn't work. The new paradigm, once the godspell is dispelled, simply frees us to go one on one with the universe and to seek directly whatever unthinkable or thinkable ultimate principle is behind it.

The Acceleration Of The Transition

It is well to be able to view the development of the new paradigm in historical perspective. By the turn of our century, scholars had become aware of the world-wide similarity of the traditions of remote antiquity in all regions of the earth dealing with the gods and their deeds. It had become incontrovertibly clear that the basic themes and motifs of human mythology were universal and even the genealogies of the gods were the same the world over. Not only were the religions of the world similar but it had also been established that much of the teaching and traditions and history of the relatively recent Hebrew religion, considered by its adherents and the offshoot Christian religion to have been revealed directly to the prophets and writers of the Old Testament, actually had been derived from the much earlier and more developed cultures of the Middle East as far back as the Sumerian civilization. The Old Testament suddenly had to be viewed as a relatively recent *Reader's Digest* type synopsis of the detailed history of the race as known and recorded by the Sumerians, Babylonians, Hittites, Akkadians, Egyptians and other cultures. These discoveries were a tremendous revelation yet deeply puzzling and disconcerting.

In addition to these discoveries there had also been major developments in the field of Psychology which were attractive to those studying myth. Freud, Jung, Adler and others had explored the realm of mythology and religion in terms of the human subconscious and had evolved psychological explanations for many of the symbols and themes that were dominant in mythology. This set the stage for an explanation of all of mythology and religion, from primitive or ancient to present, in psychological, psychoanalytic and even psychopathological terms.

The Jaynes-Campbell Syndrome

Faced with the significance of this explosive revelation and ferment, the Jesuit trained Joseph Campbell *(The Masks Of God)* set out to bring this vast information from many disciplines together to write a "natural history of the gods." He conceived of such a work as both a systematic identification and classification as well as the discovery of an evolution of the "visionary world of the gods" that might well exhibit scientific laws, indeed as the beginning of a "science of the roots of revelation." It might be termed a sociobiology of revelation. But, never reaching a point where he could acknowledge the "gods" real, as actual history, he could only hold that their source had to lie in the psychology of the minds of men, even going so far as to say that there was madness in the claims of the god-kings of Egypt. Seeing no other alternative, he could only recommend a constructive exaltation of what he considered the "mythological" portion of man's nature. Campbell's ultimate goal was to develop an encyclopedic "creative mythology" according to what he understood to be the "laws and hypotheses of the science of the unconscious." In effect he was trying to make sense out of a historical phenomenon which was full of deep contradictions and mind boggling facts and seeming madness by psychoanalyzing the mess. In doing so he had to accept the Darwinian concept of evolution from less complex forms to the more complex.

In a very real way, Campbell's conclusions involved him in a self-contradiction: at the very beginning of his work, in the first volume, *Primitive Mythology,* he asked the question, Was the source of the knowledge of the gods and the similar archetypes encountered all over the world to be found in the local projections of deity and personality on the awesome forces of nature, lightning, thunder, great storms, the wind, sun, etc. by the naive human mind of our early ancestors? Amazingly he answered, although local quaint myth may have had its origin in that way, it was a diffusion of the stunning, sudden high culture from the "little Sumerian mud garden" that was the source of "the whole cultural syndrome that has since constituted the germinal unit of all of the high civilizations of the world." If even the details of the genealogies of the "gods" were the same the world over it must have been a process of diffusion rather than local development. He went as far as to identify Sumeria as the primary mythogenic zone, a source of the origination of the universal mythic themes. But having reached that startlingly acute insight, he nevertheless had to go on to explain the gods as mythic archetypes in psychological terms — how else can you explain something that you are convinced is unreal?

Julian Jaynes, a Princeton psychologist well versed in ancient history and literature, in *The Origin of Consciousness In The Breakdown of The Bicameral Mind,* claims that, since all men previous to 1250 B.C. claimed to hear, see, communicate with, receive written information from and speak to the gods (the unquestioned assumption being that the gods were fictions) then all men previous to that time must have been hallucinating schizophrenes. Really. Read it for yourself. Impeccable logic, wrong premise. The Jaynes-Campbell syndrome, the most extreme explanation one can advance if one starts from the unquestioned assumption that the gods must have been unreal, marks the last step before the resolution afforded by Sitchin's thesis which puts the last pieces of the puzzle of our history into place.

Michael Cremo and Richard Thompson, devotees of a Vedanta teacher who suggested they do the research, have compiled a massive volume, *Forbidden Archaeology,* which documents numerous finds that would place anatomically modern humans millions of years previous to the 250,000 year time frame we are looking at for our genetic creation by the Nefilim. The Vedanta tradition speaks of humans in the remote past contemporary with primitive human and ape species. The focus of their evidence is on conclusively demonstrating that the theory of Darwinian evolution that requires the more complex to arise from the less complex is false, as have other authors. In this vein, they also document the evidence for the very strong possibility that primitive human species are still living on this planet in various remote parts of the world and present evidence of high-tech items found in very ancient strata. Their work is evenhanded and thorough and they acknowledge their sincere, long range intent is obviously to ultimately demonstrate the historical validity of the Vedanta world view in a second book.

I have carefully studied the evidence they present looking for any incontrovertible evidence that would contradict Sitchin's thesis and have found none.

The existence of advanced human civilization in the remote past that was wiped out or degenerated for whatever reason, even many times, would not contradict Sitchin's thesis. If the situation, at the point when the Nefilim arrived here and eventually needed a slave creature, was such that the most advanced human types were of sufficiently low caliber to need upgrading even to do mining as the records indicate, there is no contradiction. The Nefilim selected a humanoid type with which to fuse their genetic code or part of it, enough to raise the humanoid species to a level of intelligent competence to work as gold miners. Sitchin has indicated that the humanoid type chosen was Homo Erectus. Even if there were more advanced, physiologically identical human types contemporary with Homo Erectus 250,000 years ago, it does not, by that fact, contradict Sitchin's thesis. It does raise a question as to whether the Nefilim might have actually used a more advanced human type much closer to us to merge their genes with rather than Homo Erectus.

Another theoretical possibility is also prompted: even though there might have been anatomically modern human types available, the Nefilim could have chosen a lesser species, say Homo Erectus, as a base on which to create a slave animal for ethical or pragmatic reasons (We were described as eating the grass of the fields and drinking from the ditch when we were first invented). But, again, this does not seem logical on the basis of "why bother" if a more advanced but not up to standard type was available. And, in the last analysis, the records say nothing whatsoever about any human type then, that would have been equal to us now.

Another question suggested by Cremo's and Thompson's work is: If there were anatomically modern humans already existing on Earth, identical to us both physiologically and mentally, even to the point of being self-aware as we identify ourselves to be, when the Nefilim are said to have created us, could that mean that some contemporary humans are from purely indigenous stock and some are from the Nefilim/humanoid cross? It is at least conceivable but logically not probable: why would the Nefilim even bother if there was a species already up to standards that they could en-slave — or hire?

For whatever reason, Cremo and Thompson have chosen to ignore Sitchin's work completely in *Forbidden Archaeology;* there is no reference either in the Bibliography or the Index. I think that this is significant if only that the exhaustive 900 page work pur-ports to be a thorough coverage of the available material and the implication is that Sitchin's work is precluded as not worthy even of note. In another, explicitly Vedantic context *(Alien Identities),* Thompson mentions Sitchin's work but I can find no instance where he associates the Vedantic gods in their vimanas, aircraft, with the Nefilim. It is worth noting, however, that since the Nefilim were in the area known as modern India, the Vedanta tradition is simply talking of them under a local name. Perhaps a major con-tribution of the Vedanta tradition may eventually come from its preservation of a very detailed account of the history of the indig-enous human types previous to the Nefilim genetic intervention.

Sitchin As Hot Potato

It is one thing for Sitchin to say that it is clear that the Anunnaki/ Anakim/Neter/Nefilim were the ones who could and did set up a base on Mars and on Earth, built the Giza Pyramid as part of their second navigational landing grid, set up all the ancient high civilizations, but it is obviously difficult for others involved in specific parts of the quest to acknowledge it.

The corroboration of the evidence for the existence of the Planet Nibiru by Harrington, late head of the Naval Observatory, and his willingness to recognize the accuracy of Sitchin's work is startlingly impressive.

It is interesting that Tom van Flandern, formerly of the Naval Observatory, colleague of Harrington and searcher for Planet X/ Nibiru, denies the validity of the translated information that Nibiru was originally captured into our solar system and eventually collided with a large planet in orbit, where the asteroid belt is now, forming Earth and the asteroid belt *(Dark Matter, Missing Planets and New Comets)*. He rejects that information on the basis of his own investigations which prompt him to claim that a planet in that orbit exploded forming the asteroid belt. When asked how a planet could explode he falls back on a hypothesis that has been tossed about for some time and which is highly theoretical to say the least. Nevertheless he would agree that there is a very high probability that X/Nibiru is in our solar system. He rejects the evidence on the cylinder seal VA/243 in the East German Museum that appears to quite clearly show our sun surrounded by various size disks correctly representing all the planets in our solar system including the tenth planet, Nibiru. His reason for rejection: he has measured the diameters of all the disks and found some slight discrepancies in the diameters of some. Which means to a scale ratio of something like 1.6 billion to one on a 4500 year-old carved stone cylinder seal . . . Even the most advanced computerized precision machining does not normally produce that kind of accuracy especially in stone. It is interesting to see how different personal orientations to the same topic will cause two associated experts to radically disagree.

van Flandern has been courageous to even consider Sitchin's material in his writings. But, when one steps back for the sake of getting out of the line of fire and to get the big picture, what is becoming very clear recently is that this is not New Age politics anymore, anyone notice? It appears all too much like academic and scientific politics and ego chest bumping.

The ultimate question that all these investigators are being forced to confront is simple: Who and what was the source that is evident to us but which some claim cannot be identified? It has boiled down to four answers:

1. An advanced human civilization existed, perhaps even preceded by other human civilizations that have peaked and waned in the remote past, developed high technology and culture, and left enough around to jump-start humans somehow coming after this first civilization was wiped out or vanished. No credible explanation has ever been given as to who and what they were. Well, maybe Atlantis is a clue.

2. An advanced human civilization existed, developed high technology and culture, left enough around to jump-start humans coming somehow after this first civilization fragmented, was partly wiped out, some going to Mars and to the stars; formed groups with different agendas in conflict, manipulating us, like a dysfunctional family. Well, maybe Atlantis is a clue.

3. A race or races of alien visitors from other stellar systems has been intervening and altering humanoid development over long periods of time and has left a deposit of basic knowledge to jump-start human civilizations.

4. Sitchin's thesis. And I have not seen anyone refute Sitchin's basic thesis yet.

He never, to my knowledge, tries to discredit anyone's credentials or reputation. He will debate, disagree, reject, but will not denigrate or attack someone's character. It's obvious that he is too much of a hot potato for any of the other explanations. He is standing there with seven volumes worth of deep information about who and what all the ancient first human civilizations said, unanimously, and who that previous advanced civilization was which they received the training in technology, learning, culture and science — where they came from, what they did, where they went. **Once one gets to that question and answers it "Anunnaki/ Nefilim," the game is over.** Not only is it having to accept someone else's thesis and recognize that yours is subsumed by it but, once over the line, the paradigm shift required by the ramifications is so profound that the difficulty of acceptance is compounded by magnitudes.

Notice the percentage of Ph.D's, who are suddenly showing up in the forum? Where've they been? Waiting for the right peer signals, a shrug from their Dean, approval by the agenda makers, a request from their publisher? You have to know that, if the Ph.D's, present heroic company obviously excepted, are entering the discussion, it has already been over for years and the lodge has voted to send a delegation of experts to make definitive pronouncements about what they'll claim they knew all along and to declare the new topic as "science." But the process of coming around is torturous, so painful to even watch. And don't go too fast, don't embarrass or get ahead of the rest.

And, over and above the American side conflicts, there still is the powerful force of the official Egyptian "archaeological" department with its own agenda, jealous of its own tradition and religious ethos. And you know that Saddam Hussein is not going to stop parking his jets in the shadow of the Ziggurats to protect them as he did in the gulf War or reconstructing Babylon and other centers as symbols of proprietorship of our ancient heritage.

There is fundamental corroboration between Sitchin's paradigm and the evidence on Mars, the dating of the Sphinx and the Giza pyramid, the astronomical siting data of the great Pyramid and the topological geometry embedded therein, the astronomical evidence for X/Nibiru, the history of the gods in the Asian sector, etc. The new paradigm subsumes and completes those various pieces of discovery. I know personally many of these pioneering and, in the face of opposition and ridicule from the establishment, courageous thinkers and scientists, and find them, individually, to be persons of sincere conviction. It is sad that any less than the professional ideal prevails. Consider what it would be like if all these pioneering researchers were communicating and cooperating and working toward a common goal rather than acting like pharmaceutical researchers trying to beat each other to market with a new drug.

Growing Pains At The Leading Edge

The new paradigm requires that we do no less than rethink our entire racial world-view. *Breaking The Godspell* was my first contribution toward that end, focusing on the ramifications for religion, philosophy and science. As we move to more and more specific areas of reevaluation in this process, there is a topic that I believe needs immediate attention.

It is fascinating that the New Age Goddess movement exhibits resistance to Sitchin's thesis. Well known authors and academicians representing this focus are Merlin Stone *(When God Was a Woman)*, Maria Gimbutas (many articles: *Journal Of Indo-European Studies)*, and Riane Eisler *(The Chalice and the Blade)* among others. Their interpretations and opinions of the archaeological and historical data carry a great deal of weight because of their depth of research and scholarly approach. The reason for the attractiveness of their thesis is that it throws into perspective the neglected, even denied, status and role of women in history and points to a time in the past when, it is interpreted, there was equality of the sexes and peace among humans, looked to as a model for our time and our future. Many in the Goddess movement view the new paradigm with suspicion because they feel that it diminishes what Maria Gimbutas has interpreted as the "supernatural" element in the worship of the Goddess. But, on the basis that the truth, whatever it turns out to be, sets you truly free, I suggest closer study shows that the two paradigms mutually reinforce and the new paradigm ultimately affords an even more profound meaning to the Goddess concept.

A critical question to be addressed in this regard is whether there is hard evidence for what is interpreted as a cult of the female previous to our genetic genesis 250,000-300,000 years ago. Maria Gimbutas held that, so far, we can't see evidence for the goddess cult much more than perhaps 25,000 years ago — although she "guessed" that it might go back as far as the consensual date of the beginning of the Paleolithic era some 500,000 years ago. I see no contradiction in any form of the new paradigm by the evidence so far adduced in that regard.

The new paradigm provides an overarching context in which to attain a much more accurate explanation of several major features that are involved in the Goddess religion theory: the mythological interpretation of the evidence; the interpretation of the evidence as indication of a supernatural religion; the lumping of all particular goddesses into a single amorphous Goddess; the interpretation of the cause of the apparent "golden age" of peace among humans; the nature of the catastrophic revolution that altered the social structure to male dominant.

Because the consensus of the scholars studying the Goddess phenomenon hold to the evolutionary context, it is easy and natural to project a mythological character on the Goddess in her various forms since the implicit assumption is that the earlier we find humans in history the more naive and primitive they would be and therefore all the more inclined to mythologize. And, by extension of this interpretation of the Goddess phenomenon as mythological, it becomes easy to conceive of the goddess phenomenon as a single continuum of gradual development centered on just one Goddess, from the earliest crude Paleolithic figurines through the millennia to the very detailed images of specific goddesses in the Middle East and Crete. An end result of these interpretations as mythic projection of the primitive, naive human psyche in an historical continuum is that the individual goddesses recognized over the millennia as distinct beings, often in very different contexts and times, often with very idiosyncratic differences between them, sometimes as different spouses of different male "gods," are freely and generally taken as simply different cultural names or aspects of the Goddess interpreted as an archetype. Ultimately, the result is that the Goddess movement tends to get stuck in the Campbell half of the Jaynes-Campbell syndrome.

I believe that we can already see sufficient evidential correlation to say confidently that the basis of the goddess mother cult in the earliest times was a recognition and veneration of the Nefilim female geneticist, Ninhursag, who literally created us in the laboratory. Both the "in-law" and the "out-law" cultures would remember her equally. Gradually, over the millennia, as we became either the subjects of or at least very aware of the various Nefilim females of higher and lower social and functional rank, they also were venerated on a more local basis. Inanna, who as a member of the administrative council of twelve which oversaw the entire planet and a pilot and far ranging traveler, was very widely known to humans.

A problem lies in the fact that taking the gods as myth has allowed the various female Nefilim with their disparate personal characteristics and foibles to be lumped together as the amorphous Goddess archetype, an innocent but significant error. The recognition of the Nefilim as real allows us to see that those "goddesses" were actually individuals of an advanced culture and why, though they were humanoid, humans saw them as superior or at least in a position of superior authority. Some were highly respected and loved by humans, others less so. Some were of very high rank and authority, some were lower echelon technicians, specialists and officials. But they were Nefilim and thereby set apart from humans. Because of this amorphous melding into the goddess archetype, the less than ideally feminine characteristics of some of the Nefilim women tend to be glossed over. A single example is that of Inanna's dealings with human men whom she had killed when they refused to become her lovers. Her political ambitions caused her to manipulate in such ruthless ways that current slang would term her a "bitch on wheels." Yet she is also the one who probably gave us tantra yoga and the ideal of the fully independent, self-realized woman. Understanding the veneration of our Nefilim female rulers as both compulsory and conditioned by the relative attractiveness and benevolence of their individual personalities throws light on two other facets of human existence when the Nefilim were here on the planet.

The new paradigm provides a context in which to resolve a disagreement within the Goddess studies movement itself. One school of thought, following Gimbutas, holds that the hazy "golden age" when there was generally peace and little tendency toward social and sexual conflict was due to a matriarchal orientation: women were dominant. Others, following Eisler, would hold that this fortunate state should be attributed to a partnership of equality between male and female. Humans, in any given area, did what they were told by their local Nefilim ruler. If there indeed was a golden age of sexual equality it existed because both male and female humans were in an equally servile position: you don't get to dominate as females or as males when you are being dominated by a powerful authority. The time when male dominant groups began to overrun the scene, described as catastrophically disruptive of peaceful human society by the goddess researchers, coincides with the time when the Nefilim phased off the planet. When the cat's away . . .

The new paradigm does not denigrate the scholarly, independent and impressive work of the goddess researchers. On the contrary it affords a context in which an even more robust and digni-fied appreciation of our true history and womens' role in it. Break-ing the ancient mythic goddesspell is necessary to arrive at the more profound realization that Goddesshood is not just a high metaphor; it is literally genetic. Male dominance, even though it has a deep base in the various godspell religions focused on Yahweh who taught his male subjects to treat women as inferior, cannot survive genetic enlightenment. But we won't have to wait for those religions to disappear totally — the process is already well under way through attrition and suspicion — for it to diminish. Even though the word "obey" has been eliminated from the marriage vows only recently and the Pope is not going to accept early re-tirement easily, it is going to happen faster than anticipated. When DNA speaks, **everybody listens.**

A Potential Problem, The Inevitable Outcome

I feel it is important to sow the seed of thought concerning a potential problem in the near future. If an official announcement in any form by our or any government is made of the alien pres-ence on the planet — I believe that to be the case with regard to the little grays at least — I think it will be unfortunate if, in the heady excitement and novelty of that event, all alien presence now or in the past is lumped together and glazed over, we will miss the critical opportunity to differentiate between the intra-solar system politics of our genetic half-alien creation and a species possibly from beyond the stars. We must restore our own true history to ourselves to gain the unassailable integrity necessary to know what we are, what is good for us and not, what we can allow and not when interacting with a species very different from ourselves.

Having noted the convolutions of current philosophic and sci-entific politics which would be almost amusing if it were not for the very nasty results they have caused, we can be heartened by the positive resolution that is clearly in sight. All these currents taken into account, the vectors are coming closer and closer to the target faster and faster. The next stage will come when the scientific evidence from all the various investigative vectors begin to coalesce quickly and inexorably reach critical mass. The Mars material, the mitochondrial DNA material, the work of West and Schoch on the age of the Sphinx, the next breaking information on the existence of planet X/Nibiru, the documentary material from the find in Sippar in Iraq if we can get it out of there, perhaps even the crop circle decipherment, the announcement by the government of this country of the alien presence, etc. and, singularly, the full recognition of the master thesis of Zecharia Sitchin. At that point of critical mass the evidence will simply overwhelm the academic and scientific arenas and all scholars will be unable to ignore it.

The Ramifications For The Present And The Future

Although I have focused primarily on the current status of the new paradigm with reference to current academic, scientific and alternate explanations, my primary preoccupation remains with the ramifications for our present and future. A short summary of the resolutions and redefinitions for our present and possibilities for our future as I deal with them in *Breaking The Godspell* and *God Games,* a second book which will be finished by the end of this year, are as follows.

If we are the product of that advanced Nefilim technology, we are a mutant species with bicameral genetics, bicameral mind, a bicameral collective unconscious. Jungian psychology will have to be totally revamped.

Evolution on this planet, if we indeed will be able eventually to use that term accurately at all, was linear until interrupted by our decidedly non-Darwinian, pragmatic synthetic genesis. From that point on we have experienced a precociously rapid metamorphic process, a special case of evolution for lack of a better metaphor, under the imperative of the prepotency of our advanced

Nefilim genetic component. It is in the integration of the bicameral mind that what has been condemned as naive hallucination is
restored as our almost unthinkable history.

Institutional "religion" is a sublimation of the ancient godspell,
the subservient master-slave relationship. The Babel factor is about
to be overcome and we can reach planetary unity through the concept of our common origin and generic humanity.

Transcendental experience, in its generic form removed from
vague association with some god, magical practice, occult doc-
trines or subservient godspell ego-loss, may be redefined as par-
ticipation at the leading edge of our metamorphic self-explora-
tion/expansion as the bicameral human gradually comes to the
recognition of its true nature as Homo Erectus-Nefilimus, becoming truly sapient by that fact and passing out of the adolescence of
the race. Once free, it becomes clear that fully conscious transcendental experience may be understood as conscious dimensional expansion. I believe that we are rapidly evolving off the
Cartesian monkey-bars to habitual four-dimensional consciousness.

The genuine "occult" can now be understood scientifically to
be time-release packages of advanced technical information entrusted to us in "crash courses" in civilization until we could break
its code. Once we allow ourselves to freely begin to reexamine
these technological concepts as potentially real and valuable we
will gain much very rapidly.

Ooparts — high-tech tools, toys, artifacts, ostensibly out of
place in time are recognized as remnants of lost technology and
knowledge. Physical immortality, possessed by the Nefilim probably through genetic engineering and withheld from humans, is
seen as a collective preoccupation. It has also been sublimated to
the status of reward in the afterlife with the god or gods. If you
can't get it here you will get it there if you do as the god(s) says.
But the real technology of immortality is already on the horizon

through genetic engineering and probably through the re-discovery of the mono atomic form of gold by David Hudson, quite certainly the focus of the alchemical and some occult traditions, lost over time but remembered as the goal. Immortality will be the primary, dominant characteristic of the dawning new phase of our racial maturation, a matter of simple human dignity.

The characteristics that mark the new human are an unassailable personal integrity, relativistic epistemology, profound compassion, robust depth of informational data, understanding of the universe in terms of a full unified field, broad-spectrum competence, transcendental competition, facility in dimensional shifting, preference for dyadic operation, a profound ability to enjoy, to play the games most satisfying to generic "gods," an expanded capacity to literally have great fun creating new realities, with the primary focus on evolving habitual four dimensional consciousness and contributing to the definition of our racial evolutionary trajectory.

The new synthesis subsumes the groundswell rising to a new politic, enlightened eco-economics, re-hashed Eastern or Western mysticism, a third culture, political notions of a New World Order, spiritualized psychology, cerebral turning points, religion as we have ever conceived it. It points to a new plateau of civilization and culture fitting of the new human. And what if the Nefilim return? They were the landlords but their deed has run out. We, perhaps, should convert the SETI search apparatus into a transceiving device focused on Nibiru and let it be known that we would like to take the kids on a first visit to the grandparents place. But only if we can be accepted as an independent and mature species. If they come back throwing their weight around they are going to have a real problem with me. We should not fall back into the old godspell subservient posture in the event that the Nefilim come back any more than a mature adult should remain subservient to parental authority.

What to do after you get genetically enlightened and have broken the godspell, the effect of the ancient, subservient, looking-to-the-sky-for-daddy-to-return, master-slave attitude, the deepest dye in the fabrics of Eastern and Western culture? We will operate as our own "gods," according to our own genetic credentials, play our own god-games according to our own transcendental choices, creating our own confident realities. And play those god games in the context of relative immortality, with an unassailable integrity and racial identity which will enable us to step confidently into stellar society.

132

Jose Antonio Huneeus, the son of a Chilean diplomat and United Nations official, was born in New York and studied at the Sorbonne University in Paris and journalism at the University of Chile in Santiago. He has written extensively on science, space and Ufology for the *New York City Tribune, Noticias del Mundo, Fate Magazine,* and various ufological publications in the U.S.A. and for *Magazin 2000* (Germany) and *Más Allá* (Spain), and serves as the U.S. correspondent for large circulation magazines in Spain and Japan. He contributed scholarly papers for several MUFON symposia, the PSI Institute of Japan and at various European congresses; edited the anthology *A Study Guide to UFOs, Psychic & Paranormal Phenomena in the USSR* (1991) and co-authored *The UFO Briefing Document* (1996). He has appeared on many radio and TV programs and has lectured extensively in the Americas, Europe and Japan. He received the "Ufologist of the Year" award at the 1990 National UFO Conference and the 1991 Annual Award of the Fortean Society.

ABSTRACT

Author's introduction in the UFO field (Cpl. Valdes "time distortion" case, Chile, 1977). Zecharia Sitchin's remarks on UFOs as probes of the Anunnaki and their android servants (humanoids seen in CE-111 and CE-IV). Review of historical UFO cases in the XVI century (Nuremberg, 1561; Basel, 1566; Lepanto, 1571). Analysis of the modern UFO evidence in military terms (SAC bases alert along USA-Canada border, 1975; intrusions at Soviet missile bases in 1982 and 1989; dogfight in Iran, 1976). And from a scientific standpoint (CE-11 trace case in France, 1981; multiple witness sighting and CE-111 in Spain, 1976; landing and CE-111 in Brazil, 1969). Review of Remote Viewing data supporting scenario of artificial structures and machines on Mars (lectures by Gen. Stubblebine and Ingo Swann) and of the 1989 Phobos-2 disappearance (Psi Tech; Kiryanova). Tentative conclusions.

EXPLORING THE ANUNNAKI-UFO LINK

by

Antonio Huneeus

I began my investigation of UFOs as a science writer in 1977, one year after the publication of *The 12th Planet,* with a mysterious incident involving a Chilean Army patrol in the northern Atacama Desert. As a UFO hovered near the patrol in the desolate spot of Pampa Lluscuma, the leader, Cpl. Armando Valdes, walked toward the light and disappeared for approximately 15 minutes around 4:15 AM on April 25, 1977. At approximately 4:30 AM, Valdes reemerged behind the patrol of seven soldiers in a state of shock, with no recollection of what transpired during the missing 15 minutes. However, he exhibited a 5-day growth on his beard, and the calendar of his wrist watch marked five days in the future, April 30 instead of April 25th!

The Valdes Affair

The Valdes affair caused a furor in the Chilean press. The story was published on the front page of *El Mercurio*, the country's most prestigious newspaper, and elsewhere. The Army's Chief Command eventually issued a formal statement confirming the basic accuracy of the reports published in the press. The communiqué stated "the Army does not pronounce itself over the facts related by the members of the patrol," but acknowledged that "the versions given by the press until this moment are generally coincident with the accounts from the members of the pa-

Copyright © Antonio Huneeus, 1996

trol." I myself attempted to locate and interview Valdes in southern Chile in 1990, where he was serving with the rank of Sergeant. Unfortunately, I was unable to find him.

Chile's largest circulation daily *La Tercera* did interview Valdes in 1983, but he practically refused to talk for "personal reasons," saying that "we have to wait a little bit, but I'll talk someday." Significantly, when asked if he could now recall something about the "missing" 15 minutes, Valdes responded, "No, they are a void in my mind, I don't recall anything." He acknowledged having other experiences "related to UFO's," including a sighting of a triangular "beam of light" in Concepcion in 1977. The Valdes case thus remains unexplained and practically unique in the history of ufology.[1] We have located only one other case in China — at an Army barracks in 1975 in Yunnan — which appeared virtually identical. The Valdes case piqued my own curiosity, leading me to study the documentation accumulated by the US Air Force's Project Blue Book, the official UFO investigation from 1947 to 1969. In time, I met and interviewed the late Dr. J. Allen Hynek, Blue Book's scientific consultant and founder of the Center for UFO Studies (CUFOS), and other prominent figures in the field.

By the time I read the first two volumes of *The Earth Chronicles* in the mid-1980's and met Zecharia Sitchin in 1986, I was already well versed in the ufological field, having published dozens of articles in the USA, South America and Spain, and joined research groups like the Mutual UFO Network (MUFON), of which I am currently its International Coordinator. I was also basically acquainted with the popular "ancient astronaut" hypothesis proposed by Erich von Daniken and the Russian school of "Paleocontact." It was pretty obvious that Sitchin had developed this theory further by giving a complete picture of the so-called gods of Antiquity: who they were, where they come from, when they arrived on Earth, and why. A summary of his hypothesis of the Anunnaki from the planet Nibiru, as reconstructed from Sumerian, Hebrew and other Near Eastern sources, is not necessary here. If he is right, then the question of linking the Anunnaki with the modern phenomenon of Unidentified Flying Objects or UFOs, is a logical one. Let's see first what Sitchin himself has to say about this problem.

Sitchin's Remarks on UFOs

Sitchin dealt with the modern UFO phenomenon for the first time in his 1990 companion volume *Genesis Revisited,* which also linked the ancient Anunnaki saga with the recent enigmatic disappearance of the Soviet Phobos-2 probe to Mars. In fact, I had the opportunity of assisting him with a few ufological references in the brief UFO section where I was cited. Sitchin dealt more extensively with this matter in his paper, *The 12th Planet — Key to the UFO Enigma,* presented at the MUFON 1991 International UFO Symposium in Chicago. After providing a summary of the Anunnaki from Nibiru, Sitchin writes that, "I therefore suggest to you that the answers to the UFO enigma lie in the ancient records of the existence of the 12th planetary member of the Solar System . . ." Since the Anunnaki were really human, Sitchin then asks, "How then does one explain the claims by those who say they have seen the UFO occupants, that they do not look like us — human-like but not human? If these beings are not the Anunnaki, who are they? My answer, based on ancient evidence, is: Humanoids, robots! . . . This then is the solution I propose to the enigma of who occupies the UFOs that are reported nowadays: robots, humanoids, artificially created by the Anunnaki to man what are only scouting and exploratory missions."[2]

On March 13, 1996, I had the opportunity to conduct a lengthy interview with Sitchin as an assignment for the international magazines *Año Cero* in Spain and *Borderland* in Japan. We talked about the scientific controversy over Planet X and the return of Nibiru, artificial structures on Mars, his latest book *Divine Encounters* and, of course, UFOs. Here are some excerpts from our interview:

Z. Sitchin: "Anyone who thinks that the UFO phenomenon began in 1947 with the Roswell incident, just doesn't know history, because the experiences of mankind with so-called unidentified flying objects, which I say were in ancient times IFOs, identified flying objects, because the people in Antiquity had no doubt that they knew what they were, what they represented and who operated them. It goes back to the beginning of mankind's recorded experiences; in the new book *Divine Encounters* I even show that the cave art from caves in France or Spain that go back 20, 25, 30,000 years almost to the beginning of the spread of Cro-Magnon man, contain depictions not just of animals, all of them very realistic, [but] also include depictions of UFOs, and I give in the book a selection of 10 or 15 of them that undoubtedly are UFOs; and then of course you go to the Sumerian depictions, to the island of Crete, or the depiction of an underground silo in the Sinai peninsula, in the tomb of the Governor; so there is no doubt that it goes on and on. Now, what is the explanation for the current crop of UFO sightings . . ."

Sitchin told us that before starting to write his first book, he set himself the goal of answering four basic questions about the visitors: "First, where did they come from? Second, why did they come? Because with any technology as advanced as you are, it is an expenditure of energy, of resources, so why would they come here? The third question is, did they come on purpose, or did they just happen to come here? And the fourth question is, when did they come? Did they keep coming and going? Why? They are all answered in the first book . . . I feel that all the people who talk about UFOs — either believe in them or sighted them, had this encounter or that encounter, or were abducted, or whatever — have to answer this series of questions."

Sitchin provided some examples of close encounters of the ancient kind: "In my opinion, linking it with all the ancient evidence, and on the assumption that what was seen and witnessed in ancient times over tens of thousands of years is really the beginning of what we are seeing today, I think that the explanation is that the space base on Mars has been reactivated; not yet by the Anunnaki but by their emissaries. The whole notion that comes from the Bible of angels, as I point out on my new book, really is a translation of the Hebrew term "malakhim," which literally means emissaries. In the new book *Divine Encounters,* I show that there were all kinds of such emissaries, sometimes depicted as winged beings because of their ability to fly, not as birds, but in UFOs or plane-like contraptions in the skies of the earth; and that some of them and probably those that are reported now, were really robots, androids, and incredibly, Antonio, there is a text that I quote in the new book, a text that deals with how do you determine if the emissaries you see are living beings or androids . . . I tell of all the encounters, being in dreams, in visions, or in instances that might look as if they are episodes of the Twilight Zone programs; there are instances where the only way we, with our technology, can describe it is holographic vision or virtual reality; that somebody is taken (not only sees a three-dimensional thing [which] doesn't really exist but is shown to him) into it, like a visit to a temple that doesn't exist yet he is taken for a tour inside the yet to be built temple."

Let's now examine the UFO evidence, both historical and contemporary, under this hypothesis.

The Historical Evidence

Sitchin's *Earth Chronicles* have dealt only with ancient historical and prehistoric periods, and have not yet reached the Christian era. Meanwhile, it is generally agreed that the modern UFO era began with the first American wave in the summer of 1947. That is when the phenomenon acquired the name of "flying saucers," after the description of pilot Kenneth Arnold's daytime sighting of nine objects flying over the Cascade Mountains in Washington state on the afternoon of June 24th. It was an idea, or phenomenon, whose time had come. The flying saucers, subsequently termed Unidentified Flying Objects or UFOs by the US Air Force, were soon reported, debated and investigated throughout the world. The sightings and close encounters have continued up to this day, in varying degrees of intensity, geographical distribution, and public and official scrutiny.

One of the first questions that must be posed is whether there is any UFO activity (obviously referred historically in a different context) in the period between the birth of Christ and the present. The answer is yes. Fortunately, history provides many chronicles of prodigies, portents and other "celestial wonders," which apparently have been reported by all civilizations. The Roman era offers the figure of Julius Obsequens, a writer from the fourth century AD, who collected in his *Prodigorium Liver* (The Book of Prodigies) hundreds of strange phenomena and omens cited by previous classical authors like Seneca, Cicero, Pliny or Titus Livius. For instance, Obsequens tells of an incident in the territory of Spoletto in Umbria in 89 BC, where "a globe of fire, golden in color, fell to the earth, and ascended into the sky where it obscured the disc of the sun with its brilliance. It turned towards the eastern quadrant of the sky."

Legends of "sorcerers" from the aerial kingdom of Magonia spread during the reign of Emperor Charlemagne around 800 AD, leading to its denunciation by the Archbishop of Lyons, Agobard. With the invention of printing and subsequent renewal of knowledge, the Renaissance offers a rich collection of aerial wonders. Obsequens' prodigies were in turn reprinted and expanded by Theobald Wolfhart (1517-61), better known by his latinized name of Conradus Lycosthenes. Born in Alsace, Wolfhart was a Protestant humanist philosopher and professor at Heidelberg, who published the *Prodigorium Liver* in 1552, followed in 1557 with the Basel edition of his own *Prodigorium ac ostentorum Chronicon* (Chronicle of Prodigies and Monsters), an extraordinary compilation of strange phenomena spiced with the intense religious thinking of his time — the Christian Reformation — which took him 20 years to complete.

In 1479 a comet curiously shaped like a rocket appeared in the deserts of Arabia. One can see inside the structure small circles and a big sickle, which seems to fit the iconography of doom often given to comets in that age (Comets were not well understood until Sir Edmund Halley in the late seventeenth century). Another example: "In 1520 AD in England, at Hereford, a colossal beam of fire was seen in the sky. Approaching the earth, it burned many things with its heat. After this, it ascended into the sky again and was seen to change shape into a circle of fire." Lycosthenes was not the only collector of portents during the Renaissance. On the contrary, the field seems to have flourished in the sixteenth and seventeenth centuries, with such authors like the French Simon Goulard and Pierre Boaistuau, or the Spanish Alvar Gutierrez de Torre, who published in 1524 his *Summary of the Wondrous and Frightening Things That Have Taken Place in the World.* In his monograph "Evidence for UFOs in the Italian Past," the Florentine ufologist and sociologist Roberto Pinotti cites two Italian sources.

The first comes from the 1537 *Autobiography* of Benvenuto Cellini, the famous Florentine goldsmith and sculptor. The artist relates that, as he and a companion left Florence at night for a horse ride to Rome, "we had reached the top of a hill, and casting a glance behind our backs we both cried out at the same time: My God! What is that huge thing over Florence? It was just like a gigantic beam of fire, sparkling and shining . . ." The second incident concerns a multiple-witness sky vision a few days before the key naval battle of Lepanto on October 7, 1571, in which the combined Catholic fleets of Spain, Venice and the Roman Papal States, inflicted a crushing defeat on the Turkish Ottoman Navy. Father Alberto Gugliemotti, the official historian of the Pope's Navy, published in Florence in 1862 an interesting account of this vision:

"The night before the 21st of September [of 1571] a sign was seen in the sky, and everybody considered it a miracle. The night was quite calm and fair, with a fresh north wind and all the stars clearly visible and bright. Then suddenly a huge flaming shining pillar of fire was seen crossing the night air for a long time, filling all the witnesses with great wonders." Father Gugliemotti was an educated man from the nineteenth century, a more scientific age in which religious miracles were not so easily accepted. "Today we know we must consider," he continued, "not only wills-o'-the-wisp and St. Elmo's fires, but also fire-balls and beams of fire like this one as electric and pneumatic phenomena of the atmosphere typical and frequent during summer time." Nevertheless — he cautions — all the witnesses considered this of good omen, foreboding a great victory. They thought that the pillar of fire was showing them the way, guiding the Christian fleet in the sea as in biblical times when it guided the people of Israel in the desert.

The "pillar of fire" described in *Exodus,* in fact, has been considered by many authors as one of the best UFO examples from the Bible.

Swiss psychologist Carl Gustav Jung was one of the first to draw attention to UFOs occurring in the sixteenth century in his classic book, Flying *Saucers — A Modern Myth of Things Seen in the Skies,* where he explored the possibility that UFOs were symbolic representations or *mandalas* from mankind's "collective unconscious" (one of Jung's basic tenets). These, he reasoned, would tend to appear more frequently during periods of change and upheaval, such as our century or the Renaissance. Jung reproduced in his book illustrations from two "Broadsheets" which are preserved in the Vickiana Collection of the Central Library in Zurich. Broadsheets were the sixteenth century version of newspapers, consisting of one large sheet describing a current event with text and engravings. Thus, the awesome celestial events seen over Nuremberg on the morning of April 14, 1561, were meticulously described and depicted by Hans Glasser, a professional letter painter and illustrator from that city. An English translation from the archaic German was made several years ago by researcher Ilse von Jacobi.

Glasser's remarkable engraving shows UFOs of various types and sizes flying in the skies over Nuremberg: globe-like objects and flying crosses from which some of the globes are clearly attached; thin and long cylindrical objects and cigar-shaped tubular contraptions which also carry several globes inside; a huge spear-like dark object and finally two clearly visible plumes of smoke on the ground as if two of the objects had crashed. A brilliant Sun in the center of the picture dominates the whole scene. [See figure #1.] In Glasser's own words, this "dreadful apparition occurred on the sun, and this was seen in Nuremberg in the city, before the gates and in the country — by many men and women." Glasser describes the various "globes" and "blood red crosses and strips" and "two big rods" with small globes within. At this point, he describes a fantastic aerial battle above Nuremberg on the morning of April 14, 1561. Needless to say, there were no operational man-made aircraft whatsoever in that time, although the idea had already been developed in Leonardo da Vinci's remarkable sketches.

Picture and description from DUIST e. V. Germany. Colorslide and copy of the original broadsheet by courtesy of Dr. Edwin Slade, M.S. and Ch.E., staff scientist of ICUFON.

Figure #1

"These all started to fight among themselves," reported Glasser, "so that the globes, which were first in the sun, flew out to the ones standing on both sides; thereafter, the globes standing outside the sun, in the small and large rods, flew into the sun. Besides, the globes flew back and forth among themselves and fought vehemently with each other for over an hour . . . they became fatigued to such an extent that they all, as said above, fell from the sun down upon the earth 'as if they all burned' and they then eventually wasted away on the earth with immense smoke." We can think of no known type of natural atmospheric phenomena that could even begin to account for all of the fantastic behavior described by Hans Glasser. "Whatever such signs mean, God alone knows," he concluded.

Five years later, the skies above the city of Basel witnessed three times on the 17th and 18th of July, and again on August 7, 1566, more extraordinary celestial events associated with the sun. According to the broadsheet written by Samuel Coccius, "On the 7th of August, before and at sunrise, numerous large black spheres were seen in the sky. Suddenly they started racing toward the sun with great speed, with some turning toward each other as though in combat. Several were also seen to turn fiery red and then they vanished . . ." [See figure #2.] These fantastic accounts of aerial battles and dancing spheres around the sun seemed to occur somewhat often during the late sixteenth century. *The Prodigious and Marvelous Histories* by Pierre Bouistau, describes yet another "black squadron" around the sun over the town of Altorf near Wittemberg in the morning of December 5, 1577. These few examples, among many others recorded throughout history, attest that what today we call UFOs have been seen before. [3]

We can find no better way to conclude this historical section with the description of a remarkable celestial phenomena from none other than William Shakespeare. In the second scene of the first Act of *The Third Part of King Henry VI*, the Prince of Wales, Edward, says, "do I see three suns?" to which Richard Plantagenet, Duke of York, replies:

Figure #2

"Three glorious suns, each one a perfect sun;
Not separated with the racking clouds,
But sever'd in a pale clear-shining sky.
See, see! they join, embrace, and seem to kiss,
As if they vow'd some league inviolable:
Now are they but one lamp, one light, one sun,
In this the heaven figures some event."

The Modern UFO Evidence

A vast body of evidence on UFO reports and encounters with
entities has been accumulated worldwide in the past 50 years. Many
cases, however, are controversial and the ufological data comes
in varying degrees of reliability. UFOs can be studied from many
angles, such as military, scientific, and sociological. In 1995, I
worked on a project to distill the data to a few representative cases
that could be backed with either official and/or scientific documentation. The result was the report *Unidentified Flying Objects
Briefing Document — The Best Available Evidence,* published by

the UFO Research Coalition composed by CUFOS, FUFOR and MUFON. I was one of three authors, with Don Berliner and Marie Galbraith, who coordinated the project.

We shall review very briefly some of our report's "Case Histories" from military and scientific viewpoints. The social impact of ufology is of less importance to the purpose of this paper, although it's a topic certainly worthy of study.

There are some UFO cases that seem to demonstrate a superior military technological power to that of our own armed forces. During a two-week period from late October to mid-November of 1975, several high-security bases from the Strategic Air Command (SAC) along the US-Canada border, were penetrated by unknown objects. This declassified SAC message on "Defense Against Helicopter Assault" captured the alert mood: "Several recent sightings of unidentified aircraft/helicopters flying/hovering over Priority A restricted areas during the hours of darkness have prompted the implementation of security Option 3 at our northern tier bases. Since 27 Oct. 75, sightings have occurred at Loring AFB [in Maine], Wurtsmith AFB [in Michigan], and most recently, at Malmstrom AFB [in Montana]. All attempts to identify these aircraft have met with negative results." [4]

On the other side of the geopolitical spectrum, newly released KGB and Soviet military records show that similar incidents were taking place at missile bases in the old USSR. George Knapp, a TV reporter from Las Vegas, obtained a dossier of a Soviet military UFO collection effort between 1978 to 1988 from its former director, Colonel Boris Sokolov. The most dramatic incident was a series of sightings by several officers and enlisted men at a long-range nuclear missile base in Usovo, Ukraine, on the night of October 4, 1982. Knapp wrote that "the most disturbing account was filed by a communications officer named Davidovich. At approximately the same time that numerous military personnel say they saw UFOs dancing in the sky above Usovo, communications officer Davidovich said the launch control panel at the missile base lit up like the 4th of July. In his words, it was "spontaneous illumination of all displays," followed by a series of precise control codes, four spaces, and a control code combination. In other words, the launch control panel was being manipulated by some unknown force. [5]

The UFO Briefing Document mentions another case at a Russian army missile base in Kapustin Yar, Astrakhan Region, on the night of July 28-29, 1989. It comes from KGB files on UFOs declassified in 1991. The Kapustin Yar incident contains depositions of seven military witnesses (two junior officers, a corporal and four privates) plus illustrations of the object by the observers, and a brief case summary of an unnamed KGB officer. The sighting of a "disc 4-5 m diameter, with a half-sphere on top, which is lit brightly," lasted almost 2 hours. The UFO "moved sometimes abruptly, but noiselessly, at times coming down over ground at an altitude 20-60m." Ensign Valery Voloshin, the Officer-on-Duty, stated that "the object flew over the unit's logistics yard and moved in the direction of the rocket weapons depot, 300m away . . . While the object was hovering over the depot, a bright beam appeared from the bottom of the disc..." The KGB case summary added that, "the command of [censored] called for a fighter . . . but it was not able to see it in detail, because the UFO did not let the aircraft come near it, evading it. Atmospheric conditions were suitable for visual observations." [6] [See figure #3.]

There have been perhaps hundreds of cases in which jet fighters were scrambled after unknown traces were detected by air defense radar in many countries. Some well documented cases occurred in USA, Russia, Spain, France, Belgium, Italy, UK, Brazil, Chile, Peru, Iran, Japan, China and other countries. Some scrambled incidents resulted in virtual dogfights, with the UFO always out-maneuvering the jet. The dogfight over Teheran on the night of September 18-19, 1976, is a particularly interesting and thoroughly documented case. We have the videotaped testimony of three formerly high-ranking air force generals in the Imperial Iranian Air Force, now living in exile in the USA, and a fairly thick dossier compiled by the U.S. defense Attaché Office in Teheran and other intelligence agencies in Washington, D.C..

The Control Tower at Mehrabad Airport received calls after 10:30 PM that a UFO was flying over the capital's restricted airspace. The night shift supervisor, Hossain Perouzi, saw the UFO with binoculars, describing it as "probably cylindrical" with "two ends pulsating with a whitish blue color." Two F-4 Phantom jets

A UFO as it was seen by Ensign V.Voloshin over his army unit
(the town of Kapustin Yar) on July 28, 1989

Figure #3

were scrambled, but both aircraft experienced electromagnetic effects on their equipment. Base Operations commander, General Nader Yousefi, authorized the scrambled mission and also witnessed the UFO from the balcony of his own residence. General Yousefi described the moment of highest tension: "It was around 12 miles, we lost communication and I heard nothing from the pilots, so I was so scared what's going to happen and what happened to the pilots. I asked from the tower controller to tell them to continue their mission and see if they can get more information from the flying object... and it [UFO] was coming toward them, they try to shoot them down, when they squeezed the trigger it didn't work and the trigger was inoperative, they couldn't shoot the missiles."

A Defense Intelligence Agency (DIA) "Evaluation" enumerated the reasons why the Iranian incident was, in the analyst's words, "an outstanding report." This case is a classic which meets all the criteria necessary for a valid study of the UFO phenomenon:

a) The object was seen by multiple witnesses from different locations (i.e. Shemiram, Mehrabad and the dry lake bed) and viewpoints (both airborne and from the ground).

b) The credibility of many of the witnesses was high (an Air Force general, qualified air crews, and experienced radar operators).

c) Visual sightings were confirmed by radar.

d) Similar electromagnetic effects (EME) were reported by three separate aircraft.

e) There were physiological effects on some crew members (i.e. loss of sight/vision due to the brightness of the object).

f) An inordinate amount of maneuverability were displayed by the UFOs."[7]

Close Encounters

From a scientific point of view, UFOs offer a rich yield of data if any scientist would care to take a look. Many have indeed done so. One was the late astronomer and Project Blue Book scientific consultant, Dr. J. Allen Hynek, who coined the terminology of Close Encounters of the I, II, and III Kind. Another was Prof. Hermann Oberth, one the pioneers of the space rocket. The late Professor of Atmospheric Physics, Dr. James McDonald, the late NASA scientist Paul Hill, and the late Russian astronomer Felix Zigel, lecturer at the Moscow Aviation Institute, were other dedicated pioneers in the early scientific study of ufology. All concluded that UFOs were a real aerial phenomenon worthy of further study, most likely consisting of structured devices possibly from an advanced extraterrestrial civilization. Current scientists working on UFO research include doctors Richard Haines, Bruce Maccabee, Peter Sturrock, Jacques Vallee, Auguste Meessen, and many others.

Science needs hard data and many UFO cases offer only witness testimony, which can be unreliable at times. But Close Encounters of the II Kind (CE-II) offers physical effects left by the UFO. Burnt terrain and vegetation can be measured and analyzed according to standard scientific procedures. Perhaps the most thoroughly documented CE-II ground trace case was that of Trans-en-Provence, which was investigated by the French National Space Agency (CNES). On the afternoon of January 8, 1981, a strange craft landed on a farm near the village of Trans-en-Provence in the Var region in southeastern France. Physical traces left on the ground were collected by the Gendarmerie within 24 hours and later analyzed in several French government laboratories. Extensive evidence of anomalous activity was detected.

The witness was the farmer Renato Nicolai, 55, on whose property the UFO, shaped "in the form of two saucers upside down," landed and then took off almost immediately. Thinking that it was a military experimental device, Nicolai notified the local gendarmes on the following day. They interviewed Nicolai and collected soil and plant samples from the landing site at an alfalfa field within 48 hours, notifying the CNES Unidentified Aerospace Phenomena Study Group (GEPAN). Further collection of samples and measurements of the site were undertaken by the GEPAN team, and the samples were then thoroughly analyzed by several government laboratories. The primary investigator was Jean-Jacques Velasco, the current head of SEPRA (which replaced GEPAN in 1988). The first detailed report on the case was published by GEPAN in 1983 in its *Technical Note N°16, Inquiry 81/01, Analysis of a Trace*. [See Figure #4.]

The samples of soil and wild alfalfa collected from the landing site, as well as control samples from varying distances from the epicenter, were subjected to a number of analysis: Physico-Chemical at the SNEAP laboratory, Electronic Diffraction studies at Toulouse University, Mass Spectrometry by Ion Bombardment at the University of Metz, and Biochemical analysis of the vegetable samples at the National Institute of Agronomy Research

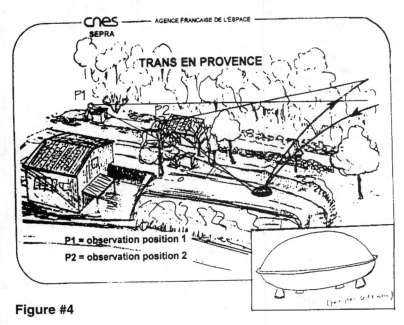

Figure #4

(INRA), among others. Some of the scientific findings outlined in *Technical Note N°16,* include: "Traces were still perceptible 40 days after the event . . . There was a strong mechanical pressure forced (probably the result of a heavy weight) on the surface . . . A thermatic heating of the soil, perhaps consecutive to or immediately following the shock, the value of which did not exceed 600° . . . The chlorophyll pigment in the leaf samples was weakened from 30 to 50 percent . . . The young leaves withstood the most serious losses, evolving toward the content and composition more characteristic of old leaves."

Most of the puzzling biochemical mutations were discovered by Michel Bounias of INRA, who described the young leaves to a journalist in 1983 with the following words: "From an anatomical and physiological point, they [leaves] had all the characteristics of their age, but they presented the biochemical characteristics of leaves of an advanced age: old leaves! And that doesn't resemble anything that we know on our planet." J. J. Velasco continues to be puzzled by this and three other unexplained CE-II's in the CNES UFO dossier. [See figure #5.] There can be little doubt that *something* capable of producing considerable physical, thermal and

cnes
SEPRA
AGENCE FRANCAISE DE L'ESPACE

CASES WITH PHYSIOLOGICAL SIGNS

ENQUIRY CASE	VISIBLE SIGNS (PLANTS)	TYPE OF ANALYSIS	LABORATORY	SUGGESTED INTERPRETATION	STUDY
CHRISTELLE 27/11/79	Grass flattened in given direction	Plant physiology	UPS Toulouse Pr. TOUZE	None	Mechanical properties of grass tissue
TRANS EN PROVENCE 08/01/81	Alfalfa leaves withered	Biochemical	INRA Avignon Pr. BOUNIAS	Electro-magnetic field Microwaves	Effect of microwaves on plants
AMARANTE 21/10/82	Grass raised Amaranth leaves withered, fruits burst	Plant physiology	UPS Toulouse Pr. ABRAVANEL	Electro-magnetic field Microwaves	Effect of lightning on plants
JOE LE TAXI 07/09/4	Birch leaves damaged	Biochemical	INRA Pr. BOUNIAS	Electro-magnetic field Microwaves	Effect of microwaves on plants

Figure #5

biochemical effects on the ground, landed on that alfalfa field on the afternoon of January 8, 1981. According to the witness, it was some kind of manufactured, disc-shaped aerial device. The French space agency was unable to determine its origin, but research on the source of these CE-II's continues at their Headquarters in Toulouse. [8]

What about the famous Close Encounters of the III Kind (CE-III), in which occupants of the UFO, the aliens, are also reported? Is there any official documentation? The answer again is yes, although the number of "entity reports" in official archives is far smaller than visual observations of lights, radar and pilot cases, etc. But nonetheless they exist. For example, a large unidentified phenomenon was observed throughout the Canary Islands on the night of June 22, 1976. Newspaper headlines proclaimed the following day that "thousands of people" had seen a "spectacular luminous phenomenon" which "lasted twenty minutes and was observed from Tenerife, La Palma and La Gomera." The most sensational aspect was the experience of a medical doctor and his taxi driver, who reported a transparent sphere with two tall entities inside.

There is a complete Spanish Air Force file on this case, comprising over 100 pages of questionnaires, evaluations, appendices, illustrations, etc. It was officially declassified in 1994, as part of an ongoing public release of Spanish Air Force UFO files. The Investigative Adjutant reconstructed the sequence of events in his final report. The first observation was made at 21:27 hrs. by the entire crew of the Spanish Navy corvette *Atrevida*. The depositions by the ship's captain and other officers and miscellaneous witnesses throughout the islands, led the Investigative Adjutant to conclude "numerous witnesses belonging to different positions and cultural strata, saw it with similar characteristics in the Grand Canary island. Therefore, the fact that a very strange and peculiar aerial phenomenon occurred on the night of 22 June is a true and proven fact, as incredible as its behavior and conditions may seem."

The Air Force investigator, however, had more problems accepting the reality of the CE-III described by some of the witnesses. Not because he questioned their veracity or suspected them of hoaxing, but simply because of the nature of the report. The CE-III's main witness was a physician from the town of Guia, Dr. Francisco Padron Leon. His deposition is the longest in the file and the Air Force also checked his background and psychological condition. Dr. Padron explained that he was called to attend a patient and was riding in a taxi to see her in the town of Las Rosas:

"As we entered the last part of the road, the car lights pointed at a slightly luminous sphere that was stationary and very close to the ground; it was made of a totally transparent and crystalline-like material, since it was possible to see through it the stars in the sky; it had an electric blue color but tenuous, without dazzling; it had a radius of about 30 m, and in the lower third of the sphere you could see a platform of aluminum-like color as if made of metal, and three large consoles. At each side of the center there were two huge figures of 2.50 to 3 m tall, but no taller than 3 m, dressed entirely in red and facing each other in such a way that I always saw their profile."

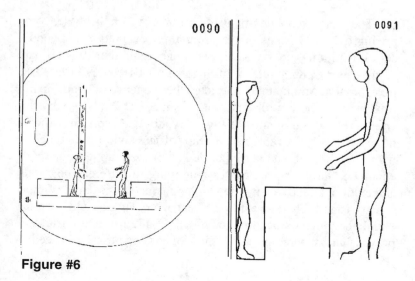

Figure #6

They were humanoid in shape with the head proportionate to the thorax and wearing some kind of head gear. [See figure #6.] Dr. Padron asked the taxi driver if he was seeing the same thing, and he exclaimed, "My God! What is that?" As the car reached the patient's house, the doctor noted that "the sphere began to grow and grow until it became huge like a 20-story house, but the platform and the crew remained the same size; it rose slowly and majestically and it seems I heard a very tenuous whistling." Dr. Padron entered the house and alerted the residents, who went outside and saw "the sphere, now high, moving slowly toward Tenerife." Dr. Padron's CE-III testimony was confirmed by the taxi driver, who also saw a craft with "two persons dressed in brilliant red inside," and by a woman relative of the patient.

The Adjutant's final conclusion was that an "Unidentified Aerial Phenomenon" was seen on the night of June 22, 1976. Moreover, it is important to note that this incident was neither the first nor the last UFO report investigated officially in the Canary Islands. On November 19, 1976, the Commanding General of the Canaries Air Zone, Gen. Carlos Dols de Espejo, and his aides, observed first-hand another large halo while flying on an Air Force T-12 transport plane. The crew of a Spanish Navy training ship and the personnel at the Gando Air Base also reported the phenomenon. The Investigative Adjutant in that case concluded his report: "If we study as a whole the three reports issued up to the present (1/75, 1/76 and 2/76), we should have to think seriously on the necessity of considering the possibility of accepting the hypothesis that a craft of unknown origin, propelled by an equally unknown energy, is moving freely over the skies in the Canaries." 9

Another interesting landing and CE-III case in Pirassununga, Sao Paulo state, was investigated by the Brazilian Air Force (BAF) in 1969. The 4° Regional Aerial Command in Sao Paulo established that year a special bureau called the SIOANI (System of Investigation of Unidentified Aerial Objects). They didn't have to go far to collect UFO reports, as a wave with dozens of landings and humanoid cases was taking place in the states of Sao Paulo and Minas Gerais in the late 1960's. SIONAI's second Information Bulletin provided a catalog of 70 such cases, including four in Pirassununga itself. An important air base is located in this town, which includes an Aeronautical Training School. Case 028 in Pirassununga on the morning of February 6, 1969:

Summary:

Small UAO [Unidentified Aerial Object, term used by BAF], with well pronounced dome, circular platform, all of aluminum-like color; in the dome, a small opening from which two crew members reportedly emerged levitating, totally protected from our atmosphere; (small — 1.40 meters; strong trunk; similar to humans; eyes out of sync); two other [beings] reportedly stayed inside. There was a reported attempt to communicate on the part of the UAO occupants (a very grave voice, hoarse)." A drawing of the disc-shaped craft was included. A confidential 2-page memorandum from a high-ranking BAF officer, entitled "Possible Landing of a UAO (or UFO) in Pirassununga — SP" [Sao Paulo], provides further details: a power and telephone blackout affected the air base during that morning, and a flying disc landed on Vila Pinheiros, while dozens of witnesses saw how 19-year old Tiago Machado tried to communicate with two humanoids that levitated out of the disc; as he rushed toward the landed craft, he was then hit on the thighs by a beam shot from a hand-held device. Machado was taken to a hospital where he was tended by a doctor, although his wounds — "two reddish large marks" — were not serious. An officer later interviewed the doctor at the hospital, who described Machado's ordeal.

The BAF investigation continued on a rapid pace, as shown by the memo: "That same day arrived from Sao Paulo, Lt. Colonel [censored] who interrogated the youngster [Machado] and approximately 300 people and, afterwards, myself; all the depositions were coincident. A Sergeant photographer took photos of the site of the possible landing . . . On the following day, I sent an airplane to Pocos de Caldas to fetch two technicians to verify the possible presence of radioactivity; negative results. On that day the bent grass was completely yellowish and exhibiting a burnt aspect, as if caused by the action of some thruster or another source of heat." [10]

These few cases (SAC bases; Usovo and Kapustin Yar; Iran dogfight; Trans-en Provence; Canary Islands; Pirassununga) are representative of a wider UFO pattern, but by no means unique. Some may ask, where are the stories of crashed UFOs and dead aliens in the custody of the US military? Or the widespread accounts of "missing time" experiences and alleged abductions of humans by the so-called "grays" so popular in current ufology? The media is full of these stories. Nevertheless, our aim here was to present the most valid official and scientific documentation for UFOs, not the most tantalizing tales. We wanted to lay a foundation with solid and reliable data, just as was done by Sitchin in his *Earth Chronicles*.

Let's move now to the final link in this brief review of UFOs and their possible connection to the old Anunnaki, their android servants, and their spacecraft.

Mars Remote Viewing

The evidence to prove all these propositions lies probably in Mars, according to Sitchin. The Martian connection and the Soviet space probe Phobos-2 incident in particular, were discussed by Sitchin in his companion volume *Genesis Revisited* and also in his documentary video *Are We Alone?* We also talked extensively about Mars in our interview. "I think that the explanation is that the space base on Mars has been reactivated not yet by the Anunnaki, just as happened in the past, but by their emissaries," said Sitchin. We discussed various Martian enigmas, from the monuments in Cydonia to the grid-like structure photographed by Phobos-II in Hydraote Chaos; and from the disappearance of the

Russian spacecraft to the mysterious malfunction of NASA's ill fated Mars Observer. "It seems to me," said Sitchin, "that somebody was there before, has been reactivating the [Mars] spaceport and probably using the [Phobos] moonlet as the artificial base, and just doesn't want us to take a close look; in other words, if we just photograph from a distance, fine, but if you come to bombard me with laser beams, forget it."

We have looked at one source of information that seems to validate almost entirely Sitchin's hypothesis of an Anunnaki space base on Mars. Unfortunately, it's not hard data like that supplied by planetary missions, but "soft evidence." We are talking of the technique known as Remote Viewing (RV), which the CIA and other government agencies recently acknowledged to have researched, developed and used operationally quite extensively from the mid-1970's, when the project got started at SRI International in California, to the end of the Cold War. The CIA maintains that it no longer employs psychics and remote viewers, although the existence of various RV projects is not in doubt. Furthermore, many of the military officers and "RV spies" have come out of the cold and proceeded to speak out about their unusual experiences through books, lectures and interview. [11]

Col. John Alexander, a US Army (Ret.) officer who worked on Psi projects first for the military and then in "non-lethal weapons" at Los Alamos National Lab, provides a definition of RV in his book *The Warrior's Edge:* "Remote viewing is the technical term for a specific psychic information-gathering process. Remote viewing is the ability of an individual to acquire information about objects or events at a distance — whether those objects or events exist in the past, present, or future." At the International Symposium on UFO Research, held in Denver in May 1992, Major General (Ret.) Albert N. Stubblebine, III, dropped a bombshell about some unusual RV of Mars. Gen. Stubblebine was the Commanding officer of the US Army Intelligence and Security Command (INSCOM), where he had the opportunity of using RV operationally on General Manuel Noriega during the conflict in Panama in

1988. After his retirement, Gen. Stubblebine became Chairman of the Board of Directors of Psi Tech, a private RV company composed of former military viewers, and was also involved with Dr. Rima Laibow's TREAT organization. In any case, the general made the following statement during his Denver lecture on "Remote Viewing as a Research Tool":

"We have looked at Mars, we have looked at UFOs, we spent some time looking at Mars . . . and if I am correct, you will be told [tomorrow] that there are structures on the surface of Mars. I will tell you for the record that there are structures underneath the surface of Mars that cannot be seen by the Viking cameras that went by in 1976. I will also tell you that there are machines on the surface of Mars and there are machines under the surface of Mars that you can look at, you can find out in detail, you can see what they are, where they are, who they are, and a lot of detail about them. Now, you can do that through RV and I defy any [space] sensor anywhere in this world today that can do that kind of analysis or give you those kinds of leads, it just doesn't exist today. Now, someday we will put a Mars station, someday we will go there, someday we will see all of this, someday we will find it, but today you do not have any capability to verify what I am saying, so I can I say it, which makes it nice."

In the Q&A session after his lecture, Gen. Stubblebine was asked to elaborate on the Mars structures. "The machinery is moving," he said, "so I don't know if it's from a leftover civilization [and] it's got a long-lived battery . . . all I am saying is that there are structures on top, there are structures underneath, there are machines on top." [12]

Another RV account of artificial structures on Mars comes from Ingo Swann, a well known New York psychic, artist and author who is sometimes referred to as "the father of remote viewing." It was Swann, under physicist Dr. Harold Puthoff, who first conceived and developed a training methodology for the government at SRI, whereby people without paranormal talent could learn how to use and control RV. At a rare lecture for the NY Fortean Society in 1992, Swann remarked that, "in 1973 we went to Jupiter with Harold Sherman. I said there was a ring around Jupiter and everybody laughed . . . 95% of the things about Jupiter turned out to be correct in 1980. Harold Sherman and I visited Mars before the NASA lander in 1976. I saw dome-like structures. I saw man-made-like structures, so we discovered buildings on Mars in 1975." The experiment was repeated in 1984, when Swann put a team of seven together, including a psychic, an intelligence officer, and trained remote viewers. Once again, "evidence of a past civilization" such as tunnels or tunneling, was reported. [13]

There is further confirmation about the so-called Phobos-2 incident of March 27, 1989 — the cylindrical "UFO" photo next to the Phobos moonlet followed by the spacecraft's mysterious malfunction — on which Sitchin reported in some detail in his video documentary, which used original footage from the Russian space agency. While this RV data was again obtained by non-traditional methods, it confirms Sitchin's Phobos-2 scenario. The Russian psychic Nina Kiryanova and the president of Psi Tech, Ed Dames, described independently from each other alien spacecraft near Phobos-2. Dames was working on "a contract that asked us to look at the demise of this Phobos-2 spacecraft, why it failed." We interviewed Ed Dames, a retired US Army intelligence Major who specialized in RV, back in 1993 for *Fate* magazine. This is what he said about the Phobos-2 incident:

"What happened to it was that it was decommissioned, it was put out of commission by two objects, one that was in orbit around Mars and one that rose up from the surface of Mars, and those were both alien objects, they were not man-made . . . They were alien devices, autonomic vehicles, and I must emphasize the act was inadvertent, it was not intentional; those spacecraft thought that the Phobos-2 was something else, and they came up and interrogated it, and their interrogation beams which happened to be directed energy beams, incapacitated it, it burnt parts of the integrated circuitry of the spacecraft, and it was strictly unintentional, it was not benign, it was not malign. They realized that it wasn't something that they were supposed to be dealing with and they both backed down, it was an accident."[14] One of Psi-Tech's sketches (usually the way a viewer first captures the information) shows a classic disc-shaped object on the surface of Mars. [See figure #7.]

Less specific in details, but quite dramatic was the vision experienced by the well-known Russian seer Nina Kiryanova on the night of March 27, 1989, when Phobos-2 malfunctioned. In an interview with A. Glazunov, Kiryanova said that she couldn't go to sleep that night, so she "tried to tune myself to this probe . . . to track it out . . . At the same instant the dark abyss around me gave way to a vertical silver well from the bottom of which a bright red sphere was coming up slowly. It dazzled me so intensely that my eyes felt pain . . . At this moment only did I notice that from this hole into space was silently moving a space ship with pulsating

Figure #7

silver glaring from its bottom like that emitted by rocket engines. The ship was the shape of a blunt-pointed bullet. I tracked it until it disappeared in the darkness, and I found myself again surrounded by impenetrable cold darkness." Glazunov noted in the reports that "three days before the failure the stellar transducer of the probe recorded an unknown object of considerable size in its field of view. In addition, a clear-cut, visible, elongated shadow was found moving on the Martian surface."[15] That material is covered in detail in Sitchin's video documentary.

Conclusions

We have come to the end of our journey from the realm of the Anunnaki to "celestial wonders" during the Renaissance to contemporary UFO research, and finally to remote viewing structures and machinery — not ours! — on Mars. What have we learned? We can enumerate a few tentative conclusions:

1. Sitchin's theory of the Anunnaki from Nibiru can explain not only the ancient chronicles of Terra, but also the modern UFO manifestation. Although final proof is not yet available, it offers a solid hypothesis that can be studied in many ways. Like all hypotheses, time will tell if it is correct.

2. Various historical records from the last 2000 years show that what we call today UFOs were also sighted at various times and places around the world, as shown by the spectacular observations in Nuremberg, Basel, Lepanto and elsewhere in the late sixteenth century, examined in this paper.

3. Contemporary ufology can be studied from different viewpoints, of which we examined the military and scientific aspects. As shown by the American (SAC alert), Soviet (missile bases in Usovo and Kapustin Yar), and Iranian

(Teheran dogfight) cases reviewed, militarily speaking, UFOs seem to exhibit a superior technology to that of our best armed forces in terms of speed, maneuverability, radar invisibility, weapons jamming capability, etc. This is one of the reasons why military and intelligence agencies from various nations have investigated UFOs.

4. From a scientific point of view, good evidence and data has been gathered by scientists both privately and officially during the last 50 years. Evidence of thermal activity was recorded in ground trace cases in France (Trans-en-Provence) and Brazil (Pirassununga). Anomalous biochemical results were detected in the French case, which led space agency investigators to conclude a "Physical phenomenon of unexplained nature" with a "High probability of electromagnetic mode of propulsion."

5. There is also ample evidence of "humanoid occupants" seen in conjunction or separated from their UFO craft. The tall beings seen in the Spanish case (Canary Islands) could leave the impression of some kind of "holographic-like imagery" produced by the phenomenon widely seen that night. On the other hand, the multiple-witness Brazilian case (Pirassununga) with physiological effects inflicted on the main witness, leaves little doubt that this was a real solid object with physical, and not holographic, humanoids. The first case could be a "technological projection" of the Anunnaki, while the second incident would apply to a physical sortie by their android servants. The UFO literature is full of other CE-III cases which we don't have space to outline here.

6. There is certainly some evidence for the apparent existence of artificial structures and machinery on Mars. This evidence consists of several visual and infrared frames taken by various American and Russian probes (Mariners, Vikings, Phobos); and the testimony of several remote

viewers that seem to confirm clearly the same scenario — both regarding the structures and the fate of Phobos-2.

The Martian — actually Anunnakian — hypothesis is one that will probably be solved within our lifetime, for the structures (Cydonia face and pyramids, grid city, spaceport, etc.) are either there or they're not. This is not an ambiguous paranormal phenomenon, but something that can be confirmed decisively, providing of course that our future Martian probes get there in one piece and are able to function . . . and the data is released to the public. A lot of "ifs," but time will tell, hopefully . . . Meanwhile, there is plenty more to study, for the historical and ufological fields are rich in data waiting to be mined.

Figures

1. Hans Glasser's Broadsheet of celestial event in Nuremberg on April 14, 1561.
2. Samuel Coccius' Broadsheet of celestial event in Basel on August 7, 1566.
3. Ensign Voloshin's sketch of UFO seen at Kapustin Yar missile base on July 28,1989; and rendition of the event by Moscow's Aura-Z magazine.
4. CNES/SEPRA Diagram of UFO landing at Trans-en-Provence on January 8, 1981; insert of craft seen by farmer Renato Nicolai.
5. CNES/SEPRA Chart of Cases with physiological signs on vegetation.
6. Sketch of UFO with tall occupants, and detail of beings, as seen by Dr. Padron in the Canary Islands on June 22, 1976; from the Spanish Air Force dossier on the case.
7. Sketch of "alien machine" on Mars made during a Psi Tech Remote Viewing of the Phobos-2 incident of March 27, 1989.

References

1. I have published numerous versions of the Cpl. Valdes affair. The most complete is "The Strange Case of Army Corporal Valdes," *NY: UFO Universe,* Winter 1993.

2. Sitchin, Z., "The 12th Planet - Key to the UFO Enigma," paper in *UFOs: The Big Picture,* MUFON 1991 International UFO Symposium Proceedings, Chicago, July 5-7, 1991.

3. Huneeus, A., "Encounters with Supernatural Beings During the Inquisition," NY: *UFO Universe,* Summer 1993.

4. Berliner, D., Galbraith, M. & Huneeus, A., "1975: Strategic Air Command Bases UFO Alert," in *Unidentified Flying Objects Briefing Document — The Best Available Evidence,* NY: UFO Research Coalition, December, 1995.

5. Knapp, George, "What The Russians Know About UFOs," paper in *UFOLOGY: A Historical Perspective,* MUFON 1994 International UFO Symposium Proceedings, Austin, Texas, July 8-10, 1994.

6. Berliner, Galbraith & Huneeus, "1989: Multiple Witness Case At Russian Missile Base," *UFO Briefing,* ibid.

7. Berliner, Galbraith & Huneeus, "1976: UFO Dog-Fight Over Teheran," ibid.

8. Berliner, Galbraith & Huneeus, "1981: Physical Trace Case In Trans-en-Provence, France," ibid.

9. Berliner, Galbraith & Huneeus, "1976: Multiple Witness Case In the Canary Islands," ibid.

10. Huneeus, A., "UFO Chronicle: The Pirassununga Close Encounter," St. Paul,Minn.: *Fate,* December 1993; for a complete English translation of the BAF memo, see my paper "A Reference Guide to Foreign UFO Documents," in *UFOLOGY: A Scientific Enigma,* MUFON 1996 International UFO Symposium, Greensboro, NC, July 5-7, 1996.

11. For a serious inside account, see Puthoff, H. E., "CIA-Initiated Remote Viewing Program at Stanford Research Institute," *Journal of Scientific Exploration,* Vol. 10, No. 1, 1996.

12. Transcript of Gen. Stubblebine's lecture on "Remote Viewing as a Research Tool," International Symposium on UFO Research, sponsored by the International Association for New Science, Denver, Colorado, May 22-25, 1992.

13. Notes on lecture by Ingo Swann on the History of RV to the New York Fortean Society, NY, December 21, 1992.

14. Huneeus, A., "Interview with Ed Dames," Parts I & 11, *Fate,* September and October 1993.

15. Glazunov, A., "Getting on the Tracks of a Silenced Phobos Probe," Moscow: *Almanac Phenomenon 1989.*

4 Bil
seed
of
Lite